GREAT BRITAIN

OR

LITTLE ENGLAND?

JOHN MANDER

PENGUIN BOOKS

Penguin Books Ltd, Harmondsworth, Middlesex
AUSTRALIA : Penguin Books Pty Ltd, 762 Whitehorse Road,
Mitcham, Victoria

—

First published 1963
simultaneously with a hard-cover edition
by Secker & Warburg

—

Copyright © John Mander, 1963

Made and printed in Great Britain
by Cox and Wyman Ltd,
London, Reading, and Fakenham
Set in Monotype Baskerville

A PENGUIN SPECIAL

S222

GREAT BRITAIN OR LITTLE ENGLAND?

JOHN MANDER

For Malcolm Muggeridge

CONTENTS

I. Introductory: Cuba Week

CHAPTER I

WHAT THE PRESIDENT SAID

ON the night of 22 October 1962, President Kennedy made 'an important announcement'. It was a solemn occasion. After those words, the world might change for better or worse; it would not be the same. For all, it was a moment of fear, of doubt, of elation; a moment of agonizing seriousness. Anything might happen; something must happen. Nobody knew for certain. All we knew was that so difficult a decision had not been taken before by a single human being.

His admirers do not claim that President Kennedy is an extraordinary man. He is not an Alexander, a Napoleon, a Churchill. He is not perhaps even a de Gaulle. The scope of the decision was extraordinary, not the man who made it. Extraordinary: because the decision affected not one army, one nation, one continent, but mankind. 'Momentous decisions' seldom seem as momentous to the contemporary as they do to the historian. In that, too, this decision was extraordinary. President Kennedy was aware of it. He did not need to raise his voice. Deliberately, unemotionally, flatly, he told his audience what he intended to do.

We, the British, were a part of his audience. But only a part. He was addressing above all his own people; the main shock and burden would be theirs. He was addressing the Soviet Union. In particular, he was addressing one man, Nikita Khrushchev, who had challenged America by putting his missiles into Cuba. He must abandon his attempt to humiliate and intimidate America or himself face humiliation. Much would hang on the outcome. Must the erosion of the Free World's power – in Berlin, in Vietnam, in Latin

America – continue? Or could 'peaceful coexistence' be made to mean what the words themselves mean: live and let live? If it could, we might not achieve the best of all possible worlds. But we might achieve an acceptable world.

Not all readers will accept the terms I have used. I have invoked a 'Free World'. I have implied that Communist intentions in Berlin, in Vietnam, in Cuba are not friendly. Many will reject these assumptions. They will point out that the 'Free World' embraces countries whose politics are a mockery of freedom. They will dispute not only the morality, but the necessity of Britain's belonging to such a community. They will deny that Communist intentions are aggressive. If they are right, President Kennedy's action was not only wicked, but foolish. He risked our lives not only in a bad cause, but also in bad logic. For it is their contention that Soviet designs are not offensive, but defensive.

I make no claim to be unprejudiced. I regard this view as mistaken, disastrously so, both for Britain and for the world. I believe that the British reaction to Cuba Week revealed what many have long suspected: that a gulf now divides the British view of the Cold War from that of our allies. It is arguable that the British outlook is right; perhaps it is saner, less hysterical, more reasonable. But the view can be questioned; and it is the purpose of this book to do so. Britain did not always have this attitude towards the Cold War. In Greece in 1944, in Berlin in 1948, in Korea in 1950, the British view differed from the American (at times by being more militant); but there was an underlying identity. I shall try to discover how, in the ten years leading up to Cuba, this identity came to be eroded.

It is a theme of some topical concern. How did the divergence come about? What factors, internal or external, combined to make this the distinctively British view? The period is too close, we are too enmeshed in its polemics, for an objective historical account. Nor am I a professional historian. Yet the problem is acute: it affects Britain's whole stance in the world. What has been John Bull's prospect in the past? What ought it to be in the future? To many my account will seem overdrawn; to some, grotesquely wrong-headed. Few will agree with all that I have to say. But I have put my cards on the table: I would ask the reader to be patient.

CHAPTER 2

WHAT JOHN BULL THOUGHT

WHAT did Britain think during Cuba week? By quoting from editorial comment, from the utterances of public figures, I shall let the evidence speak for itself. The actual events that led up to Cuba week are familiar; I shall not reiterate. Nobody now doubts that the Russians had missiles in Cuba. What is interesting is why people doubted it at the time. It is not in dispute that the Russians were lying during September and October when they assured the Americans that offensive weapons would not be installed in Cuba. Nobody now doubts – though many did at the time – that President Kennedy's action was carefully calculated, that the Russians were never put in a position from which retreat would be unacceptable. Certainly, we have the advantage of hindsight. We did not know of the Kennedy–Khrushchev correspondence. But Kennedy's caution was plain from the action he took; he ordered a blockade, not an invasion. The evidence on which we would base an assessment now was not lacking during Cuba Week itself. The facts were plain: they were only not believed. Or, if believed, wrong conclusions were drawn. It is because the Cuban issue was uniquely clear-cut that its lessons are uniquely educative.

The President's speech was broadcast by the B.B.C. at midnight, British time: too late for any but the briefest comment in next day's papers. Nevertheless, comment gave an indication of the way opinion was moving.

He [President Kennedy] has surprised more than his enemies by the announcement which he made last night. (*Telegraph*)

12

... if Mr Khrushchev has really begun to build offensive missile bases in Cuba, he has done so primarily to demonstrate to the U.S. and the world the meaning of American bases close to the Soviet frontier. (*Guardian*)

Even if the bases *are* in fact being built, President Kennedy surely would have done better if he had first reported this to the U.N. Security Council ... (*Herald*)

His excuse for this act of a bully won't bear a minute's examination. (*Worker*)

The only papers, on the first day of the crisis, to support the President without reservation were the *Evening Standard* and the *Express*.

That first day was to set a pattern. Apart from the Beaverbrook press, no British paper was prepared to give the American action unqualified backing. We should contrast this with the general, though not universal, support for Kennedy in the French, German, and American press. The initial British reaction was not violent rejection. It was rather a policy of wait-and-see: grudging, incredulous, apprehensive. On the second day, *The Times* expressed a lukewarm approval, but concluded.

In spite of all the differences in Russia's and America's records and motives ... there is just enough similarity in the siting of some of the bases to cause the question to be raised ... they may consider a bargain whereby each does away with a forward base or two.

This idea – that Turkish bases might be exchanged for Cuban – was seldom absent from British editorials during Cuba Week. Rejected in the *Telegraph*'s second-day editorial, it met elsewhere with a ready response. The *Herald* wrote:

Khrushchev has taken no warlike action against these bases in Britain, Italy, Spain, Greece, Turkey, and Pakistan ... Castro could equally claim that any Soviet bases in Cuba are defensive.

On Wednesday morning, the *Guardian* wrote, imputing a new motive to the President:

The effects of President Kennedy's action may well be felt long after the American elections next month . . . In the end the United States may find that it has done its cause, its friends, and its own true interests little good.

On Thursday, the *Guardian* also took up the idea of an exchange, hinting that Cuba's loss might be Britain's gain:

If their intended prize is the bases in Britain and Turkey, then something might be done. . . . As a first step it might be arranged that the Soviet bases in Cuba and the American missile stations in Turkey are dismantled simultaneously under U.N. supervision.

By Saturday, *The Times*, with a show of reluctance, had added its voice:

Comparisons between the Cuban and Turkish bases are hotly and quite rightly resented by most Americans. The history and the whole context are indeed different. Even so a case can be made for banishing offensive missiles from each base.

A pattern was now established. On the extreme left, the *Worker* thought Kennedy's ultimatum

an act of madness unequalled in modern times. Having seen these pictures it is obvious why the U.S. did not consult its allies before it plunged the world into this terribly dangerous situation. For only the lowest of toadies would have agreed in advance to support the U.S. proposal of risking nuclear war because of photographs such as these.

But it was evident that the majority of British opinion – from the *Herald*, through the *Guardian*, to *The Times* – was not behind President Kennedy's action. The exceptions remained the *Express* newspapers, the *Telegraph*, and the *Mirror*.

How far was Conservative and government opinion behind the President? Lord Altrincham, in Thursday's *Guardian*, found a 'fatal similarity' between Kennedy and Eden:

Like Eden he is vain, ambitious, fundamentally lacking self-confidence. . . . Driven into an orgy of demagogy . . .

(In the same column, a week later, Lord Altrincham hand-somely withdrew these remarks.) No doubt Lord Altrincham reflected one section of Conservative opinion. But on the Right resentment was directed against Kennedy's toughness with his allies, rather than against his toughness with the Russians. Nevertheless, there do seem to have been doubts in the highest circles of America's wisdom. The *Observer*'s Political Correspondent wrote, on the following Sunday, that

the American Ambassador, by all accounts, left the Prime Minister angry, depressed, and uneasy. No one tried at all to con-ceal the Government's resentment. Britain, it was emphasized, was carrying no cans for Kennedy, not this time anyway. . . . There are still nostalgic feelings in Whitehall for the statelier days of Ike, the days when the man at the other end of the White House telephone (if he wasn't playing golf) was an old and trusted colleague, who had commanded armies instead of a motor-torpedo-boat. Did these young men, it was being asked on Tuesday, know what they were doing? . . . It [the Cabinet] just hasn't trusted Kennedy-on-Cuba since the melancholy episode of the landing at the Bay of Pigs. . . .

Later, Mr Michael Foot was to suggest that the Prime Mini-ster had been considering a declaration of British neutrality. This appears to have been based on a misinterpretation of a report in the *Guardian*, subsequently disclaimed by its author. But the acute lack of enthusiasm reflected in the *Observer*'s account was evidently not far from the truth.

By the end of the week, then, the following pattern had emerged: Kennedy's action had met with qualified assent on the further Right, scepticism in government and moder-ate Conservative circles, and almost unanimous disapproval in the papers of the Liberal centre, the moderate and the further Left. A strong statement against President Kennedy's action, and what amounted to a demand for British neutral-ity, was signed by a group of dons: A. J. Ayer, H. J. Eysenck, Joan Robinson, A. J. P. Taylor, Richard Titmuss, Raymond Williams. It was later revealed that this statement had been signed by as many as 600 university teachers. Whether this reflected intellectual opinion in the country is not certain. But it already seemed to require more courage, in the prevailing climate of opinion, to support the American action than to oppose it.

The response of the weeklies (published Friday) and of the Sunday press (published before Khrushchev's withdrawal became known) strengthens this impression. Alone among the weeklies, the *Spectator* gave unreserved support to the President. The *New Statesman* was divided: Kennedy's 'irresponsible warmongering' was denounced, but an editorial saw mitigating circumstances, should the photographs prove genuine. (It later became known that the photographs had been released, at Mr Macmillan's request, to convince the British public of the need for action.) Its Political Correspondent, however, wrote that America's attitude to Cuba

had always seemed a mixture of the hysterical, the petulant, and the absurd, and there could hardly be a worse course for a British government to have to uphold.

Tribune took the same line. Under a banner headline THE WAR CRIMINALS, it told its readers:

Election fever is rising in the United States. It may well be that Kennedy is risking blowing the world to hell in order to sweep a few Democrats into office. . . .

Comparing the President with Hitler, *Tribune* continued:

No British Prime Minister, we trust, not even the present one, would order the turning out of the Palace Guard on evidence from so unreliable a source as the C.I.A.

If this response from the traditionally anti-American Left was predictable, the response of the right-wing *Economist* was more surprising:

Some Americans, but we hope not Mr Kennedy, may be tempted to interpret these developments in what could well be a dangerously wrong way. They may be persuaded that by forcing a showdown over the shipment of Russian arms to Cuba ... the U.S. has achieved that decisive victory in the 'contest of will'. ... The theory that represents Mr Khrushchev as needing only to be convinced of American willingness to go to war, and he then will negotiate in earnest, is too facile.

Of the 'serious' Sunday press, the *Sunday Telegraph* and the *Sunday Times* followed the line of their weekday namesakes. The *Sunday Times* appeared to express the same doubts among Establishment opinion that had been voiced by *The Times* and the *Guardian*. The following week, however, it had this to say about its Cuba Week editorial:

Last week in its leading article the *Sunday Times* argued that the Cuba crisis should be settled by negotiation. That the Cuba–Turkey offer was worth considering, and that the U.S. would not be justified in invading Cuba after that offer had been made ... By Sunday afternoon this had been partly overtaken by events. ... A few readers have written with the advantage of hindsight, to ask if we withdraw the leader. We do not. ...

On that Sunday itself, with the outcome of the crisis still in the balance, the *Observer* had written:

The chief blame ... lies clearly with Russia ... But an invasion of Cuba now would be madness. ... For the United States, too, must share some of the blame for the present situation. ... Is it really insulting to suggest that the U.S. should give up her missile bases in Turkey as Mr Khrushchev has now proposed ... He [President Kennedy] himself has shown courage in the highest degree. But the greatest courage and the greatest self-sacrifice may be for the Americans to give up their emotional longing to 'win' the Cold War. ...

Already, on Saturday morning, the *Guardian* had gone a good deal further:

The words coming out of the State and Defence Departments have an ominous ring. They suggest that if the Russians do not at least stop work at the missile sites with the existing equipment bombing or invasion may begin. ... If it does come to that the

British government should make it clear that it must vote against the United States in the United Nations just as the Americans voted against us at Suez. *There are times when ranks must be broken, if the cause that unites them is not to become meaningless.* [My italics.]

This was, evidently, a demand for British neutrality. Thus, by the end of Cuba Week, the pattern of opinion had hardened. Certain sections of opinion – the right-wing press, the *Mirror*, and some individual commentators – had rallied to the President. But at the end of the week a larger section was rather more critical of President Kennedy, and more disposed to conciliate Khrushchev, than at the beginning. A week later, in the *Observer*, Sir William Hayter was to remark: 'The British public, or some of it, lost its head.'

The conclusion is difficult to deny. But it is less important to discover what the British public thought during Cuba Week than to discover why. Why did British opinion so conspicuously fail to support its major ally? Why were American and Russian intentions, in article after article, *equated* – as if Britain were a neutral? Why was America blamed for wanting the Soviet missiles removed, but Russia not blamed for putting them there? How did nuclear disarmers, opposed to the spread of nuclear weapons, come to cry 'Hands off Cuba' – thereby defending Castro's right to possess them?

I believe a clue to what happened can be found in the thinking of groups often considered to belong to the fringe of serious opinion. I refer to Lord Russell and the Campaign for Nuclear Disarmament. Consider these two cables, dispatched to the two world leaders by Lord Russell during the crisis. To President Kennedy:

YOUR ACTION DESPERATE. THREAT TO HUMAN SURVIVAL. NO CONCEIVABLE JUSTIFICATION. CIVILIZED MAN CONDEMNS IT. WE WILL NOT HAVE MASS MURDER. ULTIMATUM MEANS WAR. I DO NOT SPEAK FOR POWER BUT PLEAD FOR CIVILIZED MAN. END THIS MADNESS.

To Prime Minister Khrushchev:

MAY I HUMBLY APPEAL FOR YOUR FURTHER HELP IN LOWER-
ING THE TEMPERATURE DESPITE THE WORSENING SITUATION.
YOUR CONTINUED FORBEARANCE IS OUR GREAT HOPE. WITH MY
HIGH REGARDS AND SINCERE THANKS.

There is surely a family resemblance between these attitudes
and those exhibited in British press comment. Perhaps few
British people would have called President Kennedy 'mur-
derous' or 'worse than Hitler', or written

You are going to die because rich Americans dislike the government
Cubans prefer. Do not yield to ferocious and insane murderers.

But if Lord Russell exaggerated, he exaggerated sentiments
with which many were half in agreement.

It seems that the Cuban crisis brought out the latent
neutralism and anti-Americanism of a large section of British opinion. It would be wrong to speak of 'an emotional
spasm'. It was rather an adventure in logic. During Cuba
Week, the implications of much that had been said and done
in Britain over the past decade came home to roost: Britain
showed herself a half-way neutral nation. Lord Russell is not
to be blamed for taking the argument to its conclusion. I
disagree with him, but I admire his logic. I do not want
Britain to go Lord Russell's way. But I believe Lord Russell
and his friends have seen the implications of these attitudes
more clearly than most.

Is my picture of British opinion during Cuba Week too
harsh? Is that how others saw us at the time? I offer the
reader two American views of British conduct during Cuba
Week. On 2 November, Mr Max Freedman cabled to the
Guardian from Washington:

Senior officials of the Kennedy administration are saying that
the British government was by any test the most helpful ally, and
this fact will not soon be forgotten by those who have to make
major decisions for the United States.

On 12 November, Mr Joseph Fromm cabled this report to
U.S. News and World Report from London:

An American in London sometimes wonders whose side Britain is on. Among Britons who influence opinion and shape policy, the first reaction in the crisis was to justify Russia for putting missile bases in Cuba. These Britons were sceptical of U.S. charges against Russia, critical when U.S. didn't consult Britain or let the U.N. handle the whole crisis. Surprisingly few influential people saw establishment of Red missiles in Cuba as a challenge to the West, a threat to U.S. and therefore to Britain. Fear of nuclear war explains much of this British attitude. In fact, this fear has given rise to some desire to contract out of the Cold War in the hope Britain might stand aside if U.S. and Russia came to blows. This is also true: the British believe in compromise. It was this spirit Hitler exploited at Munich. During the Cuban crisis, it appeared that many of Britain's most influential people have yet to learn the lesson of Munich. As a leading editor told this correspondent privately the other day: 'The moral for America is this: don't listen to Britain in a crisis.'

I ask the reader to judge which is the better fit.

II. Britain at Large

CHAPTER 3

COUSINS IN ARMS

'WHOSE side is Britain on?' Mr Fromm was to ask, recollecting Cuba Week in tranquillity. Was the answer, perhaps, *neither side*? Did Britain, in effect if not in fact, opt for neutrality during those days of crisis? Had public opinion put itself, in effect though perhaps not in intention, on the side of Khrushchev and Castro, in its vociferous demands for negotiations, mediation, and an immediate end to the blockade? One thing British opinion plainly was not: pro-American. In Britain, this has already been forgotten, but elsewhere it is likely to be remembered. That week, Americans followed their allies' reactions with some care, nor did it escape them that German and French opinion showed more resolution than British. If any one day saw the death of Britain's 'special relationship' with America it was Tuesday, 23 October 1962. The day has already been acclaimed as a watershed in East–West relations. That is possible, though optimistic. But that it was a watershed in relations between Britain and America is certain. Who can doubt that the Skybolt affair, Nassau, and Mr Acheson's speech at West Point were influenced by it? Let me make it clear – though it should not be necessary – that I am not, in blaming Britain, taking America's part. On the contrary: I believe there are features of the Cuban crisis that argue against too close a dependence on American power. There are, I believe, good arguments why Britain (or Britain-and-Europe) should maintain an independent deterrent. The question is not whether Britain should be 'pro-American' or 'anti-American'. Britain will continue to be intimate with America, as she has been in the past. But the relationship will be different. Exactly what form it will take in future is not easy to say. Should Britain go it alone? Must she choose between Europe and America? Could she become the leader of the non-aligned nations? We shall discuss these possibilities. But let us first set down what the relationship has been in the past.

The reasons for the past intimacy of Britain and America were psychological and strategic. The psychological bonds are obvious enough. American democracy is the child of British democracy. America's religion, literature, and law spring from British roots. Yet politically these bonds are less decisive than they seem. The common features of American and British democracy may be obvious to us now; they were not always obvious in the past. America used British liberal traditions to castigate British imperialism. And why not? From our perspective, the critique seems justified. More, the censure is double-edged: the same liberal anti-imperialism can now be used against America. It is clear that the psychological bonds between Britain and America were always ambivalent. This is not to dismiss either British or American crusading-for-democracy, in hot war or cold, as mere hypocrisy. But nations do not go to war unless other, more material, interests are at stake. Such interests have had their place in the long strategic intimacy since the British last burned Washington in 1812.

From 1815 until 1914, the major strategic fact in the world was the supremacy of British naval power. Britannia ruled the waves. Britain maintained this power, in the first place, to protect her interests: her world-wide trade, her Indian, African, and Australasian Empire. It would be as foolish to condemn Pax Britannica as to allow nostalgia to see it as a golden age. Pax Britannica did great good; it suppressed the slave trade, destroyed piracy, multiplied the wealth of nations. But we did not establish it for reasons of philanthropy: we did it for our own good. It meant that all other seafaring nations must come to terms with the dominant power: to that extent, their freedom of action was circumscribed. British power 'tolerated' the Dutch in Indonesia and the French in Madagascar; both ultimately depended on British good will. No nation depended more on this tolerance than the United States of America. Though she was almost self-sufficient in raw materials, and had a vast expanding internal market, trade with advanced industrial nations was vital to her. Like Europe, she required Indian tea, South African diamonds, Brazilian coffee, Malayan rubber. If Britain had the power to starve her of this trade, why did she not do so? Why did she not punish the rebellious subjects of King George? The answer is plain. It was more in King George's interest to safeguard his capital in America and increase its returns. A tacit bargain was struck between King George and rebel America: Canada remained British; America acquiesced in British supremacy at sea; Britain abstained from interference in the affairs of the Thirteen Colonies. No treaty records this bargain, yet it determined Atlantic strategy for a century. The Monroe Doctrine (invoked during the Cuban crisis) was a development of it: Britain and the United States were resolved not to tolerate the interference of any third power in the Americas.

For a century this strategic intimacy persisted. In what proportions were a common democratic ideology and sheer power-interest mixed in that relationship? Here, the cynic and the idealist fall into opposite and equal errors. The cynic sees only *raison d'état*; the idealist sees only ideology. No doubt both were present. But few nations allow ideological sentiment to silence *raison d'état*. (Whether this is still true in a totalitarian age is a question highly relevant to this book.) Certainly, in the unwritten understanding between Britain and America, ideology played second fiddle to *raison d'état*. When Canning called in the New World to redress the balance of the Old, he spoke in the interest of 'anti-colonialism'. Yet Britain, busily building her own Empire in the east, even while helping to dismantle the Spanish Empire in the west, was hardly a suitable champion of colonial liberation.

Britain perceived that to create an independent Latin America would serve her interests better than to bolster the Spanish Empire. In the United States, the ideological motive was powerful; in Britain it was of secondary importance. After Canning, Britain's economic predominance in Latin America was similar to that of the United States today. Again and again, the pattern of British self-interest paralleling American ideology recurs in the relation between the two nations. Ideologically, America remained critical of British imperialism until the age of Roosevelt. Yet Britain and America fought together in 1917. The partnership between them was shown then to have more material foundations.

During the nineteenth century, the United States was the sleeping partner. But her experience of the world was moulded by her unwritten treaty with Britain. For young America isolationism was psychologically attractive: it expressed her contempt for the old European order. But physically isolationism was possible only so long as the seas were wide and the Royal Navy ruled them. During the middle years of the nineteenth century, this was not apparent. America's freedom from 'entangling alliances' appeared providential and eternal. What now seems a fluke of geography was to America part of the natural order of things. The British had burnt Washington in 1812, but it was the Kaiser's submarines which first taught America that the Atlantic could be a highroad as well as a dyke. That she could stand aside from Europe's quarrels seems not America's luck, but her merit. Her sense of a providential dispensation was also inherited from Britain. The English Channel, like the Atlantic Ocean, encourages illusions of isolation and immunity. Because of it Britain has been able to dispense with standing armies. She has also tended to see warlike exchanges between states as deviations from a norm, not as manifestations of never-ceasing conflict. Britain bequeathed these attitudes to America, where they were intensified by America's greater remoteness from Europe.

It is a legacy America does not find it easy to forgive. What are America's new militancy, her post-war contempt for neutralism, but a reaction against the isolationism and neutralism that long informed her own view of the world? And has not Britain, by an ironical stroke, inherited America's abandoned posture? I shall argue that this is indeed what has happened. But first we must see how the older relationship, in which America was the sleeping partner, came to an end. It would be tempting to set one date, one moment of awakening from the isolationist dream. And if one date were to be set, it would have to be Pearl Harbour: 9 December 1941. Yet, in fact, America's assumption of world-wide responsibilities was a lengthier process. By the beginning of the twentieth century, America had become deeply involved in the Far East. She had acquired Alaska from Russia and the Philippines from Spain. She had declared her Open Door policy for China. She had mediated between the belligerents in the Russo-Japanese War. It was the same nearer home. By building the Panama Canal, by detaching Texas from Mexico, and Cuba and Puerto Rico from Spain, she had begun a policy of direct intervention in the affairs of Latin America.

The decisive break was President Wilson's commitment of America to the Allied cause in 1917. The course of America's first intervention in Europe and her subsequent and disastrous withdrawal are familiar. From our perspective America's début as a world power must seem oddly under-rehearsed, an awkward prelude to a drama that lies twenty years ahead. Yet it was serious enough at the time. It created in America a new generation, radically affected by this first confrontation with power politics. When the drama began in earnest, after Pearl Harbour, it was this generation that held the reins of power. Yet the disaster of America's withdrawal from Europe between 1920 and 1940 is hard to exaggerate. 1917 had shown that France and Britain could no longer stand alone against any power which dominated Central Europe. What had been demonstrated then did not become less true after Versailles. German power would recover: Western Europe would not be able to resist Germany alone. Britain and France knew this, and the knowledge helped to undermine their will to resist Hitler. America bears her share of responsibility for what happened at Munich.

Aroused, America does nothing by halves. After Pearl Harbour, American potential was mobilized to the limit: the war doubled her economic capacity; Britain and Russia were fed, armed, and clothed. Except on the Russian front and at Alamein, America bore the brunt of the war to destroy German and Japanese power. There was now no spot on the globe where American influence did not make itself felt. By 1945, America had become in fact what she had long been potentially: top nation. In this country, the implications were not immediately understood. We had 'stood alone' in 1940: that was what Britain preferred to remember. The decisive shift in world power after Pearl Harbour went unremarked.

The First World War was to destroy the myth of maritime supremacy, the myth which had moulded the traditional Anglo-Saxon view of the world (it is one reason why General de Gaulle is suspicious of Anglo-Saxons). Yet history suggests that there is something freakish and short-lived about maritime power. Great empires can be quickly built up on a basis of sea-power – and as quickly struck down by a hostile land-power. Sea-powers suffer from a false sense of security. They fail to protect their home-base because they imagine a land-lubber enemy cannot build a fleet. Yet in the struggles of Sparta against Athens, of Rome against Carthage, of Islam against the Crusaders, it was land-power that triumphed. Only if the home-base is impregnable, as Britain's long appeared to be, does the rule not apply. That Britain built the world's greatest empire is not surprising: what is astonishing is that she held it for so long. Even so, the contrast between the fate of the Russian and the British Empires is instructive. In 1914 it seemed that

Britain's was an empire on which the sun would never set. Today it is gone; yet Russia's empire is intact, indeed stronger than in 1914. Britain's empire partook of the freakishness of all maritime empires. What was the fate of Athens and of Carthage? When the crash comes, it comes quickly and leaves little behind.

How little, even now, do we grasp what happened between 1939 and 1942? In three short years the whole material basis of an empire was swept away – not less irrevocably than that of the Austrian and Ottoman Empires between 1914 and 1918. Naturally, the decline of empire was not as sudden as these dates suggest. War compressed into a few months a process that had begun fifty years before, with the rise of American and Japanese sea-power in the Pacific, and of German and Russian land-power in Europe. Nevertheless, the effective collapse was very sudden. In 1939, Britain controlled a larger portion of the earth's surface than at any other time in her history. She was the dominant power in Africa, in the Middle East, in India, in south-east Asia, and in Australasia. So far only the Irish Free State (if we exclude the United States itself) had seceded from her empire. Directly or indirectly, Britain bore the responsibility for the lives of some 600 million people – a third of the human race. It was an empire sustained by a gigantic bluff. The Royal Navy was no longer unchallenged. The world's major land-powers were either temporarily weakened – like France and Germany – or had temporarily withdrawn from the arena – like Russia and the United States. Nevertheless, in 1939 Englishmen might almost be forgiven for thinking that theirs was an empire on which the sun would never set.

The end was swift and painful. In 1940 Hitler was on the point of invading England. By not doing so he made his first fatal error. It is true that Britain's evident will-to-resist was a deterrent; but it was not the only deterrent. Even then, Britain did not stand alone; America and Russia were in the background, important factors in Hitler's calculations. It is important not to exaggerate Britain's wartime role. Of

Alamein it has been said that it was the last great battle
fought by the British empire. But at Alamein Britain's
resources in men and machines were greatly superior to the
enemy's: a superiority which would have been inconceivable without Germany's commitments on the eastern front.
Germany fought the African campaign with her left hand.
Again, Britain contrived to hold India after Singapore, her
'impregnable' eastern sea-base, had fallen to a landward
attack. If Japan had had no other commitments, she could
have pushed on into India, across Burma and the Bay of
Bengal, without serious difficulty. What saved India was the
diversion of resources forced on Japan by American successes in the Pacific. The passing of maritime supremacy from
Britain to America dates from the Battle of Midway in the
spring of 1942. Most Englishmen have probably never heard
of this American battle. Yet it destroyed the basis of their
empire for ever.

These facts do not diminish Britain's role in the struggle
against Japanese militarism and German Nazism. But
Britain's post-war troubles spring in part from a false estimate of her wartime role. It is therefore important to get the
facts straight. After Midway, it was on American sea-power
that the British presence in India, in south-east Asia, and in
Australasia depended. At Alamein, it was thanks to Russian
land-power that Britain held Africa and the Middle East.
In a sense, the British appeasers of Hitler had been right.
War against Hitler would destroy the British Empire;
whereas a pact with him might guarantee it for decades –
at a price. It was Churchill, despite himself, who presided
over the dissolution of the empire. Naturally, the great
Allied victories were not interpreted so pessimistically at the
time. Yet they changed the British–American relationship
out of all recognition. In 1939 British power was the shield
behind which America took shelter from the world; by 1942
it was American power which was the shield for Britain and
her Empire. There is at hand simple and striking proof of
this. When Australia and New Zealand signed the Anzus

defence pact with the United States in 1951, Britain was not invited. Britain might not realize the implications of Midway; Australia and New Zealand did.

Pearl Harbour destroyed American isolationism, probably for good. But isolationism's seven devils, expelled from the American body politic, were not to be cheated: they entered into the body of her transatlantic ally. America had once thought herself exempt, thanks to the Royal Navy, from the struggle for power. Britain now developed the same symptoms. Britain's withdrawal was a gradual process, and for the most part unconscious. It differed in different areas of the globe and at different times. It was a process as complex as the Empire itself. Nevertheless, there is a pattern discernible in these withdrawal symptoms. This pattern is one of the keys to the malaise that has affected Britain since 1945. Let me point to one of its superficial manifestations. It was in Asia that the collapse of British power was most complete. It is there that the withdrawal symptoms have been most obvious. Consider the Anzus pact: it severed the old strategic ties on which the Empire had been based. There were still strong ties of trade, of language, of general sentiment between Australia and Britain. But the old power-relationship had gone. Our cousins at the antipodes are hardly to be blamed. They were merely realistic. But what of the sentimental neo-imperialism of those who equate the Commonwealth of today with the Empire of fifty years ago? They mistake the shadow of power for its substance. One wonders: is the collapse of empire perhaps more damaging to the head than to the members?

An American, reading our newspapers, would gain certain impressions. He would be struck by the extent of comment on Africa and the paucity of comment on Asia. Yet which is the more important? Asia has a population of one and a half billion human beings, one half of the human race; Black Africa scarcely more than a hundred million. Africa's problems are important; they are not irrelevant to the Cold War: but it is in Asia that the menace of Chinese expansion will have to be met. To an American, the disproportion would seem self-evident. The guerrilla war America is fighting in Vietnam is widely reported in the American press; in the British press hardly at all. Even the struggle against the terrorists in Malaya, the one striking British success in the Cold War, never aroused an interest comparable to Sharpeville, Suez, or Katanga. The reason is evident: Britain exercises an influence in Africa that she cannot hope to have in Asia. But the withdrawal symptoms are there, and to an outsider unmistakable. It might strike him that Britain's clashes with America on Far Eastern policy – on the recognition of China, on the anti-Communist struggle in Laos and Vietnam – spring rather from indifference to Asian affairs than from active disapproval. Britain has withdrawn from Asia: the British public no longer feels responsible.

I am not concerned to argue the merits of recognition or non-recognition of Mao's China. I am not implying that American policies have always been wise, or will prove wise in the future. I imply only that American policies are more *responsible*. They are the policies of people who will have to carry those policies out. Much in the British press must strike the outsider not as wrong, but as *irresponsible*. There would be nothing surprising in this if it were not for the change that it represents in British attitudes. It is only because America bears the true responsibility – and is known, subconsciously, to bear that burden – that public opinion can indulge in isolationist attitudes. What has happened is that Britain and America have exchanged roles. Britain has inherited America's self-righteous isolationism. America now belabours Britain with the arguments with which Britain once belaboured an isolationist America. There would be something comic, if it were not also tragic, in this remarkable transposition.

CHAPTER 4

BLOODY FOREIGNERS

FRENCHMEN are foreigners; Americans are not. It is irrational that Englishmen feel this way, but they do. The Englishman abroad is not arrogant, as Continental legend has it, but shy. The Englishman is not at ease with the Frenchman, the German, or the Italian. The foreigner is an infringer of taboos. He talks too much; he is serious when he should be light, light when he should be serious; he has wit, but no humour; he is intelligent, but he shows it; he mistakes modesty for lack of *esprit*. Of course, the Englishman's foreigner, like the foreigner's Englishman, was always a caricature. But it was not ignorance on the Englishman's part – he knew Europe better than foreigners knew England. The Englishman judged his fellows socially, according to the rules of a game. Foreigners had different rules; they embarrassed him. With Anglo-Saxons he did not feel embarrassed. The shared language was coincidental. At worst, Americans were country cousins; Frenchmen were always bloody foreigners.

The distinction is not scientific. But it is empirical; it is the way Englishmen feel. Let us add that it is also stupid, silly, and barbaric. Yet it is not easily changed. I shall argue in this book that we are unlikely to shake off our famous malaise until we feel ourselves to be Europeans. That implies something more than 'joining the Common Market'. The problem is this: Europe and Britain have shared certain experiences since 1940, but they have reacted to these experiences differently. Various as they are, the Common Market countries share certain reactions; and these set them apart from Britain. These reactions have little to do with the more

31

familiar abstract distinctions: Roman Law and Common Law; Rationalism and Empiricism. I am speaking of the reactions of ordinary people in Europe to the upheavals of the past generation. These reactions have not been well understood in this country. Frequently, indeed, they have been maliciously misunderstood. Yet we shall have to understand them if we are to come to terms with Europe. General de Gaule, unfortunately, is often three parts right.

He is right, I believe, in taking seriously the existence of a world Anglo-Saxon community. He is right in suspecting that the English have not in the past felt themselves part of Europe. Like many Europeans, he would point to strategic rather than cultural reasons for this sense of isolation; to that traditional policy of balance-of-power, which appears as unscrupulous to Europeans as it appears moral to Anglo-Saxons. General de Gaulle inclines to the traditional assumptions of the Continental anglophobe. That is why, in a Europe divided between anglophiles and anglophobes, it is important to understand them. His strategic suspicions of Britain amount to this charge: that Britain's relation to continental Europe fatally resembles that of America towards Europe as a whole. In the previous chapter we discussed this situation in reverse: America inherited from England her false sense of isolation. It is true that modern weapons have reduced the value of both Atlantic and Channel as defensive ditches. De Gaulle is aware of this. But de Gaulle's suspicions are not directed against present British and American military dispositions. His doubts are directed towards the future. What he fears is the mentality to which the existence of those ditches gave rise. During the war, he remarked to Churchill: 'Britain is an island, France the cape of a continent, America another world.' Churchill does not appear to have disagreed.

Today de Gaulle predicts an eventual return to isolationism, a withdrawal to Fortress America. This withdrawal will be forced on America, he thinks, not only by her own isolationist instincts, but by the facts of the case. Already, he maintains, there are signs that America would not bring her nuclear potential to bear, should Russia attack Western Europe. At first sight, de Gaulle's reading of Cuba Week is paradoxical: Kennedy's action was both a triumph and a warning. America is alert and strong; he has made plain his admiration for Kennedy's boldness. But Cuba Week is also a warning: in calling Khrushchev's bluff Kennedy has devalued all promises of nuclear support by major powers to minor ones. Cuba Week wears a double face: in so far as France identifies with America it inspires confidence; in so far as France identifies with Cuba it undermines confidence. Yet all America's allies are in this ambiguous situation. De Gaulle would add that Western Europe is no longer the inferior of the United States in economic and military potential, as she was fifteen years ago; except in the field of nuclear capability, the differential is no longer so steep. This points to a gradual American withdrawal from Europe over the next ten years. It is necessary for France both to exploit the bargaining possibilities inherent in this situation and to organize Europe's nuclear defence before the withdrawal is complete.

If de Gaulle is right, his logic is also applicable to Britain. If logic requires France to have an independent deterrent, it requires Britain to have it too. The prospect may not be welcome; but the logic is not easy to refute. Let us postpone our discussion of the British independent deterrent until later.

What, then, is this 'non-European mentality' with which de Gaulle charges the Anglo-Saxons? Literally, there is no such thing as a 'European mentality'. There is nothing to prevent the Common Market Six claiming Charlemagne and Napoleon as their forebears; but the claim will be received with scepticism. On the other hand, the existence of a 'European mentality' in post-1945 Europe is not a myth. De Gaulle, of course, is a late-comer to the feast. His interpretation of that mentality is not that of 'Europeans' like Jean Monnet or Robert Schuman. Indeed, the most articulate

'Europeans' regard his outlook as a distortion of their ideals. Nevertheless, de Gaulle's interpretation must be taken seriously. Whether we like it or not, it is the interpretation with which we shall have to deal.

He might put the matter like this: what distinguishes the European political mentality from the Anglo-Saxon is its sense of perpetual involvement. The European thinks in terms of land-power; the Anglo-Saxon in terms of sea-power. The European state is confronted, throughout history, by the same geographically adjacent, potentially hostile ring of opponents. The Anglo-Saxon lacks this sense of perpetual tension, for an island has no frontiers; the ocean, a no-man's land, is the islander's element. Naturally, Britain has not stood aside from Europe's turmoils, but her reaction has been different. Indeed, it is almost a question of reaction-time. European countries had standing armies; Britain did not. Of course, Britain too raised great armies and intervened in Europe's wars. But there was a difference between such armies and those of Europe: the difference lay in the time available for mobilization. A standing army is an army in a state of permanent mobilization. The Anglo-Saxons, with their maritime supremacy, could count on sufficient time being available in which to prepare. A Continental power could not. This sense of initial security has moulded the British and American political mentality. In Britain's hesitations over the past twenty years, de Gaulle sees clear evidence of this. How else explain Britain's abolition of conscription? How else explain the Anglo-Saxon obsession with air-power, that modern extension of the maritime heresy?

These views will seem parochial to the English reader. If these are the General's views, let Britain have no place in his old-fashioned, inward-looking Europe with its power-politics and militaristic ambitions! That is what de Gaulle would expect an Englishman to say. It would confirm his suspicions. For the gulf is real and not to be wished away. The 'European mentality' may be a myth. But there is no mistaking the difference between the mentality of de Gaulle and the mentality of a Gladstone, a Woodrow Wilson, a Baldwin, or a Roosevelt. Greatly as they differ, none could have been a Frenchman. The mind of de Gaulle is, in the true sense, Macchiavellian. It is the traditional mind of Europe: the mind of Talleyrand, Metternich, and Bismarck. It is a mentality untouched by that Anglo-Saxon utopianism which – he would say – lay behind the 'betrayal of Europe' at Yalta. De Gaulle has never forgiven Yalta. On the day Hitler attacked Russia, de Gaulle is said to have remarked: 'The problem now is to deal with the Russians.' The story may be apocryphal. But it is credible of de Gaulle as it is not of Roosevelt; though it is, of course, credible of Winston Churchill.

To de Gaulle, the European is a realist. Unlike the Anglo-Saxon, he cannot afford to be otherwise. The Anglo-Saxon thinks of war and peace as discontinuous states. War is one thing; peace another. The European follows Clausewitz's famous maxim: to the Anglo-Saxon, war is always the unforeseen contingency. That is why the first battles are lost and the last – with luck – customarily won. But for the European the first battle may well be the last. The Anglo-Saxon does not examine the credentials of peace too closely; peace is a signal for general relaxation. The Anglo-Saxons were disgusted, after Versailles, with French 'playing at power-politics'. In fact the French were merely concerned for their security. The Anglo-Saxon is innately optimistic and utopian. That is why the Anglo-Saxon is both more ruthless in war than the European and more complacent in peace. To the Anglo-Saxon each war is the last. De Gaulle does not believe in the moderation of the Anglo-Saxon. The Anglo-Saxon is a utopian extremist. It is the European who is the political realist.

Of course, it is a caricature. But there is enough truth in it to be disturbing. The two mentalities are not arbitrary: they are rooted in different historical experience. In Britain's case, Dunkirk confirmed this sense of difference. Like Cuba,

Dunkirk was an ambiguous historical experience. On the one hand, it strengthened Britain's sense of involvement with continental Europe; but it also weakened it. That Britain had been so nearly conquered encouraged her to cooperate with post-war Europe. But that Britain had not been conquered, thanks to her Channel, sharpened her sense of distinction from Europe: it encouraged isolationism. Which lesson was the more powerful? I believe the second lesson has made the deeper mark on our thinking. Britain has paid a heavy price for the rhetoric suffusing her finest hour.

De Gaulle is not to be identified with Europe any more than Europe is to be identified with France. But de Gaulle's hostility to the Anglo-Saxons should not be put down to his treatment at the hands of Roosevelt and Churchill, shabby as it was. That is to underestimate the General's character and intelligence. Nor can his attitude be dismissed as chauvinism. The distinction in his mind between the European and Anglo-Saxon mentality is not mere fantasy. Later, we shall discuss what certain English intellectuals in the thirties thought about the Soviet Union under Stalin. The most famous example is the Webbs' *Soviet Communism: A New Civilization?* How do we explain these intellectual follies? Could they 'have happened anywhere'? I am not speaking of Communists, but of English liberal idealists. It is true that illusions about Soviet Russia were widespread in Europe at the time, but if we are honest we must admit that the wishful thinking that led English liberals to condone Stalin's crimes, while condemning Hitler's, could not easily have happened elsewhere than in England. De Gaulle's view, I take it, is that of all approaches to communism Anglo-Saxon liberal idealism is the most disastrous. I happen to believe that de Gaulle's traditionalist view of Communist behaviour is equally mistaken. But it is true that Anglo-Saxon – and particularly British – liberalism has a unique record of wishful thinking about totalitarianism. Which mentality, then, is more appropriate to the world of Cold War politics in Cuba, Berlin, Vietnam, or

India – the Anglo-Saxon or the European? Which does this world more resemble: the Europe of Bismarck, Metternich, and Talleyrand, or the open seas and the broad prairies that moulded Anglo-Saxon experience? There are no more empty spaces in the world. There is now no escape from involvement. The Anglo-Saxons have come up against an irremoveable frontier which they cannot destroy without destroying themselves. De Gaulle would argue that the old-fashioned, power-political mentality of Europe is more appropriate to this reality than the broad horizons of Utopia.

It is ironical that de Gaulle, who claims to speak for the new Europe, should have consistently opposed it until his return to power. In judging its prospects, he made the same mistake as our own politicians. The story of the British misjudgement is now familiar. Churchill, in his Zürich speech of 1946, had helped to call the Strasbourg Council of Europe into being. He did not wish Britain to take part in a European federation, but he proclaimed such a federation to be a British interest. Out of office, eminent Conservatives had appeared to take the Council seriously. The Labour government, on the other hand, despite Bevin's support for the Marshall Plan and Western European defence, was little interested in Strasbourg. Britain was instrumental in ensuring that the Assembly should have only consultative powers. The second phase of the struggle to *faire l'Europe* came in 1950, when the Schuman Plan for the integration of the Franco-German coal and steel industry was proposed. Britain was invited to be a founder-member. She refused, on the grounds that her nationalized industries could not be put under international control. This was a major error. For, unlike the abortive Council of Europe, the Schuman Plan was an immediate success, and provided the basis for the later success of the Common Market.

The third phase, the proposal for a European army, was also British in origin. Churchill proposed it at Strasbourg in the summer of 1950. Back in office, however, Churchill and

his colleagues neglected their brain-child. They refused the
European army any permanent British contribution. The
outcome was the French Assembly's rejection of the concept
in August 1954. Without Britain's participation, France was
not willing to risk so intimate an alliance with Germany.
The collapse of the European Defence Community led to
the admission of West Germany into Nato. Ironically – since
it revived a national German army and compelled Britain
to commit four divisions to Europe – this solution was actually less satisfactory to both France and Britain than the
concept of a European army. The fourth phase of European
integration was the setting up of Euratom, and of the
European Economic Community, at Messina in June 1955.
The British public and the British government had taken
the collapse of the European army to be the end of the
European movement. By 1956–7 the British government at
least began to see its mistake. The Common Market was
going to succeed. Negotiations began for a Free Trade Area
to complement – or, as the French maintained, to undermine – the Common Market. This was the situation de
Gaulle inherited when he returned to power. Fearing the
disruptive effect on the Community of this scheme, on 14
November 1958 he ordered the negotiations with Britain
to be broken off.

We have witnessed a repeat performance. Nor is it clear
what course Britain should now take. But what is the most
striking feature of the story of Britain's post-war relations
with Europe? In the early fifties, European aspirations were
contemptuously dismissed. Ten years later, Britain embarked
on a humiliating attempt to come to terms. What had
happened in the meantime? It was no doubt less sudden
than it appeared. Yet how did French fear of the Germans,
which destroyed the European army in 1954, so abate by
1958 that the French could dispense with Britain as a coun-
terweight? Mysteriously, between these two dates, despite
Suez, despite Algeria, the French had recovered their
national self-confidence. The reasons for this are not

altogether clear. The revival of confidence, particularly of economic confidence, preceded de Gaulle. Indeed, it preceded the Common Market and coincided with a period of great political confusion. Apparently, the quiet efficiency of French economic planning had already created the basis of a new mood of self-assurance. By 1958, in any case, the French had lost their fear of the German businessman as well as of the German soldier – at a time when anti-German fears were growing in this country. By the late fifties it must have looked to the outsider as if Britain was losing self-confidence as fast as France was regaining it.

But it was not only France. A mistake many British commentators made was to see as national what were really European phenomena. There was much talk of a German miracle. That miracle certainly occurred. But it can now be seen in context. It was part of a general revival of post-war industrial activity, which set in later on the Continent than in Britain, and later in Italy and France than in Germany. The growth-rate of Italian and French industry is now higher than the German. All three are higher than the British rate. What is striking is not the contrast between Britain's economy and Germany's, but between Britain's economy and Europe's. Britain has been the victim of her optimism. The reason for the neglect of Europe by Attlee, and then by Churchill, was Britain's temporary economic buoyancy. Britain had recovered more quickly than her neighbours after 1945. Between 1952 and 1954 she benefited from a favourable shift in the terms of trade. During the renewed economic floundering of the middle fifties, British interest in a now expanding Europe revived. Yet the French ultimatum of November 1958 made little impression on public opinion. 1959, an election year, brought with it a further short-lived burst of prosperity.

If we do not inspire confidence in the General, it is not difficult to see why. Nor is it altogether easy to blame him. But how did British self-confidence come to be sapped after the middle fifties? Or is that to post-date the change? Did the process start in 1947, when Britain found she could no longer sustain a great-power role in Greece, Turkey, and Central Europe? Is Britain's present malaise a recapitulation of the thirties, with Communism rather than Nazism the object of appeasement? Were those foreigners right who saw in Britain's appeasement of Hitler a shell-shocked world-weariness, the legacy of Passchendaele and the Somme? Some of these questions must remain rhetorical. To others I hope to suggest answers in the course of this book. Meanwhile, it may be instructive to take the opposite case. Why should Europe, so deeply humiliated between 1939 and 1945, have fared better in the long run than Britain in the post-war world?

I suggest three reasons. The first has to do with the differing effects of decolonialization on Britain .and Europe. Against the usual view, I believe Britain to have suffered in the process far more than her fellow-colonialists on the Continent. She has severed her ties with empire more decorously. But in exchanging the fact of empire for the fantasy of Commonwealth she has seriously impaired her sense of reality. Europe's sense of reality, sadly diminished during the inter-war period, has been sharpened by the traumatic events of the past generation. Continental Europeans have experienced, in addition to violent loss of empire, violent conquest by foreign armies, and the prospect of violent revolution within their frontiers. In all three respects European experience has differed radically from British. There is no denying that it has been a more unpleasant experience. But it is arguable that its ultimate lessons have been more profitable.

Once again, we are often misled into seeing in national terms what is a European phenomenon. We think of Germany as a vanquished nation, France and Benelux as victor nations. We assume that the memories of 1940 have been overlaid. But the European's attitude to the war is more ambivalent. He was both vanquished and victor. France did defeat Germany; but Germany also defeated France.

Italy shared Germany's victories; but she was beaten before the end. The Benelux countries shared the Allies' triumph; but not before tasting the full bitterness of foreign conquest and occupation. Only the Anglo-Saxon powers were spared these experiences. Thus the bonds between the victors are supplemented, and at times supplanted, by the bonds between the vanquished. The experience of the Six with international Communism was similar. France, Belgium, and Italy experienced an attempt at insurrection during the great strikes of autumn 1947. Germany has been confronted with the existence of a separatist Communist state within her own boundaries. A European may still be a convinced Communist. But he cannot today be a fellow-traveller, as so many Englishmen and Europeans were before 1939. That is possible only in countries that have not experienced Communism at first hand.

At first sight, these terrible experiences do not seem the best soil for the growth of political self-confidence. Indeed, that was the view President Truman took when he launched the Marshall Plan in the summer of 1947. Europe then seemed virtually on the point of collapse. It was also the attitude taken by the Labour Government when it held Britain aloof from Europe after 1945. We can see now that it was a mistaken view, and one for whose conceit we have had to pay dearly. But if Europe's slow recovery of confidence, given American aid, was predictable, Britain's slow loss of confidence was not. It is the seesaw effect that needs to be explained. Certainly, there were material advantages in being the loser in the war. Factories had to be re-equipped. Once re-equipped, they were more efficient than the old-fashioned plant on which British firms relied. A similar law of obsolescence operated in other fields. Too many socialists still speak of 1945 as a social revolution. It was nothing of the sort. The desperate need to re-equip, replenish, and restore the broken European economies blew away more cobwebs than Labour's 'social revolution'. Wartime destruction forced millions to build a new life. Europeans were prepared to put up with worse conditions, to work longer hours, to expect less immediate reward than ourselves. They did not consider the world owed them a living. Again, Britain's tragedy was her optimism. Britain adopted the role of old-man-down-on-his luck; Europe the role of young-man-on-the-make. The former role is more entertaining; the latter is more rewarding. The latter at least has beginner's luck. The former presents a loser's face to the world. He puts on a good show, but is not really confident. To redeem his fortunes, mysteriously lost, he is tempted to gamble. That was the cruel portrait of Britain John Osborne painted in *The Entertainer*.

CHAPTER 5

WHITE MEN'S BURDENS

WAS it a fair portrait? Had John Bull become Mr Osborne's Entertainer, whose jokes nobody laughs at, whose advice nobody heeds, by whom – in short – nobody is any longer entertained? After Suez, it began to seem plausible. Not since the Boer War had Britain been so humiliated publicly, and made the butt of men with black skins, yellow skins, brown skins – and even white skins. It was a traumatic moment. But what was Britain's reaction? Was Suez Britain's moment of truth, the moment when her post-war weakness was brought home to her, compelling a new realism in her outlook? Or did the shock of Suez cause the national organism to contract into its shell, to withdraw from foreign contact, to cultivate its nostalgia? Perhaps we are still too close to the event. Certainly, the reaction was not simple. On the Right, it appears to have been twofold. On the one hand, in the name of realism, conscription was abolished and priority given to Britain's independent deterrent. On the other, the public was encouraged to forget its troubles: 'it's *Great* Britain again,' we were told, and 'you've never had it so good'. At the time, the 'new realism' in defence was widely welcomed. Soothing syrup was not quite the tonic for a bruised and bewildered nation. But at least it prevented us from nursing our resentment and brooding over our past.

On the face of it, the reaction of the Left was very different; at a deeper level, very similar. The Sandys White Paper of spring 1957, which abolished conscription and adopted a policy of massive retaliation, gave rise to the

Campaign for Nuclear Disarmament. It was fashionable when the movement began (and it is fashionable now) to make light of its political significance. I do not agree. The Campaign for Nuclear Disarmament seems to me the most spontaneous, virile, and sincere political movement Britain has seen since the thirties. Those who saw only bearded weirdies and political beatniks on the road to Aldermaston missed the point: that was the cap of the iceberg. Among the new left-wing generation after Hungary and Suez it was rare to find firm opponents of C.N.D. The strength of uni- lateralism was that those who were not for it did not care to speak against it. We are all pacifists, if the alternative is to count as warmongers. It was only when the movement won a majority at Scarborough and challenged the authority of the Labour leadership that Gaitskell fought back. Within the year, unilateralism had been defeated. Frustrated on the political plane, the Committee of 100 led the movement into non-violent but illegal agitation.

Yet it would be a mistake to measure the influence of C.N.D. by a party-political yardstick. Like the Peace Ballot of the thirties, its impact was out of all proportion to its strength. Baldwin, in the 1935 general election, thought it prudent to take into account the popular pacifism of which the Peace Ballot was one expression. I believe Mr Macmillan acted in much the same way when he went to Moscow. He was taking into account a deep popular pacifism of which C.N.D. is merely one expression.

Unilateralism was never easy to pin down. It was always intellectually ambiguous. The essence of the movement might be described as 'nuclear' pacifism. The arguments that 'absolute' pacifism applies to warfare in general were applied to nuclear warfare alone. The intellectual weakness of this position is evident. How is moral pacifism divisible? Where is the line of legitimate destruction to be drawn: at 1,000, at 100,000, at 100,000,000? The problem was never honestly confronted. Absolute pacifism would seem intellec- tually sounder. And many unilateralists were in fact absolute pacifists. But absolute pacifism too has its snags. Many people, not themselves pacifists, are careful to say that they 'respect' the pacifist position. I would be more sure of this if I knew what it involved. The argument seems to me valid only so long as the pacifist himself 'respects' his position. An honest pacifist must admit that, in refusing to fight against Hitler, he made Hitler's victory more likely. This may sound harsh; but surely it is realistic. The absolute pacifist has made his decision, he has preferred the voice of his conscience to every other obligation. Well and good. But does not the logic of this demand an abstention from political activity? The absolute pacifist can advocate non-violence for himself. But has he the moral right to advocate non-violence for his countrymen – knowing, if he is realistic, what the conse-quences must be? Perhaps he has. But personally I 'respect' the pacifist who admits he has not. And this has some bear-ing on the question of nuclear pacifism. As private individ-uals it is certainly possible to 'respect' nuclear pacifists; indeed, they have shown great courage. But must we 'respect' them as political demonstrators shouting 'No war over Berlin' or 'Hands off Cuba'? Here, they are recommending a policy to their fellow-countrymen whose assumptions they do not openly declare. For the nuclear pacifist has already made his choice: *any* course of events is preferable to the use by his country of nuclear weapons. But this is some-thing with which the majority of his fellow-countrymen probably do not agree. They do not accept that there are *no* circumstances in which nuclear weapons should be used. They are not prepared to pull out of Berlin 'because the alternative is nuclear war'. They are acting on different assumptions from the nuclear pacifist.

In practice, both nuclear and absolute pacifists take a weaker line altogether: they argue that the threat of aggres-sion is *not really there*. I confess that in this case I do not find it easy to 'respect' the pacifist position. Here is what Bertrand Russell (then, as in the First World War, an absolute pacifist – a position he was to abandon in the

Second World War) had to say about Britain's defence and
the Nazi menace in his *Which Way to Peace?* (1938):

> When disarmament is suggested it is natural to imagine that
> foreign conquest will inevitably follow. . . . This is a mistake as
> the case of Denmark shows. . . [The Danes] are defended by their
> very defencelessness . . . if they [the foreign states] did not [leave
> us alone] we should have to yield without fighting and we should
> therefore not arouse their ferocity. The consequences both to our-
> selves and to the world would be infinitely less terrible than the
> consequences of a war, even if it ended in complete victory . . . if
> a German were to write a history of our rule in India he would
> easily establish to the satisfaction of the Germans that our love of
> democracy is humbug. I do not say that all this would be just, but
> it would be no more unjust than the view that many British anti-
> Fascists have of Germany.

The drift is familiar: how much of the 'liberalization' of
Communism we hear about reflects a similar wishful thinking? It is clear that the logic of absolute pacifism resembles
that of nuclear pacifism. The nuclear pacifist recommends
policies to his fellow-citizens whose assumptions he does not
always openly declare. Thus, the consistent nuclear pacifist
cannot advocate a non-nuclear policy for Britain and yet
rely on American nuclear protection. He must be prepared
to advocate surrender rather than wage nuclear war. Again,
the argument is a harsh one. But the thoroughgoing nuclear
pacifist, like the thoroughgoing absolute pacifist, should be
able to admit its logic – even if it implies, as for the absolute
pacifist, something like an abstention from politics. In fact,
nuclear pacifists are seldom so consistent. Indeed, in evad-
ing the argument, they are often led to a highly immoral
conclusion. They find themselves arguing that Americans
may handle weapons which would pollute the hands of mere
Britons. The alternative is to abandon unilaterally the moral
logic of their argument. Nuclear weapons, they will then
argue, are not bad in themselves. It is British possession of
them that is bad. British control of nuclear weapons is bad,
not in any absolute sense, but for political reasons. This, of

course, is a perfectly reasonable proposition (though not, I happen to believe, a correct one). It is also why much of the moral fervour of the movement has evaporated. That Britain should abandon her independent deterrent is now widely accepted. For unilateralists, however, this has two equally undesirable implications. They must abandon, on the one hand, the nuclear pacifism that was the moral force of their movement. On the other hand they must accept, as staunch anti-Americans, a far greater degree of dependence on the United States than Britain has hitherto known.

No wonder unilateralism has tended to exalt emotion above reason. But to point to its fallacies is not to dismiss C.N.D. politically. It remains, I repeat, by far the most significant political movement Britain has produced since the war. Even in terms of practical politics it has left a deeper mark than is usually admitted. Ten, twelve, fifteen years ago, few voices were raised against the manufacture of atomic weapons by Britain. Labour, whose post-war government had initiated the process, was no less committed than the Conservatives. Yet today the greater part of public opinion rejects the independent deterrent as an expensive and dangerous chimera. The government's own position is ambiguous. Britain's future deterrent is to be both 'fully independent' and 'fully integrated'. It is a remarkable shift of opinion. True, the technical difficulties were not understood ten years back. But would such a volte-face have come about without six years of agitation by C.N.D.? Is it wrong to assert that the public, alerted to the significance of nuclear war, has taken the same escape-route as C.N.D. itself?

For it is, surely, an escape. Whether or not Britain owns an independent deterrent, she is a member of an alliance which relies on nuclear weapons. We may detest the fact; but if we deny it we are open to a charge of moral cowardice. Politically it is far from irrelevant, I believe, whether Britain does or does not have an independent deterrent. But morally it *is* irrelevant. Britain participates in the nuclear equation by being a member of the Western alliance. I do not myself think that the distinction between absolute and nuclear pacifism is valid: it is all or nothing. But one certainly cannot salve one's conscience by relinquishing the burden of guilt and decision to another member of the alliance. There is, of course, one obvious way out: let Britain have no part in such an alliance. Not surprisingly, from the beginnings of C.N.D., neutralist voices began to make themselves heard. By the time of the 1960 Scarborough Labour Conference political neutralism was explicit: a country committed to unilateralism could no longer be a member of Nato. Soon, nuclear disarmers would be demonstrating against the Common Market as a 'Cold War grouping', and in favour of British neutrality in the Cuban conflict. Here, evidently, a more straightforward escape from the moral dilemma was being attempted. Britain must not only renounce her own nuclear weapons, she must renounce complicity in the balance of power depending on such weapons. A neutral, non-nuclear Britain, it was argued, would have nothing to lose but the chains of Nato membership. In compensation, the moral leadership of the non-nuclear, non-aligned world would be hers for the taking. Once more, John Bull would take up the White Man's Burden.

I do not think the conclusion follows from the premiss. But up to a point the argument is logical enough. If the moral case against the bomb is accepted, Britain has no alternative but to go neutral. (But with this difference: many neutral states would like nuclear weapons of their own if they could afford them. Britain would be unique in not wanting them. Nor does neutrality necessarily imply non-nuclear status; the opposite, as the debate in Sweden and Switzerland has shown, might be the case.) I believe that this logic informed much British neutralist feeling during Cuba Week. Of course, the moral case against the bomb is one thing, the political and strategic arguments against a British deterrent quite another. Nevertheless, the two arguments have become confused in the popular mind. Britain's renunciation of nuclear weapons, instead of being a confession of technical defeat, is presented as a virtuous act. Nuclear capability – that new White Man's Burden – would become the exclusive responsibility of the United States. Other factors – resentment at American or European 'usurpation' of Britain's power – have contributed to this incipient neutralism. But the 'moral' arguments for neutralism have greatly enhanced its appeal.

Cuba Week suggested that the neutralist mood is more widespread than most people suspected. It is worth, therefore, having a look at what a neutral Britain would be like. Earlier, I said that the reactions to Suez on the Left and on the Right were more similar than surface appearance suggested. I said also that the C.N.D., despite its superficial political weakness, was really the cap of an iceberg. Let me, at this point, combine the two hypotheses. I suggest that the post-Suez isolationism of the far Right and of the far Left were really two caps of the same iceberg. Both types of isolationism had, after all, a great deal in common. Both were strongly anti-American – though not for the same reasons. Both were anti-European; the far Left because Europe was 'reactionary', the far Right because Europe was a rival. Both were pro-Commonwealth: the far Right because of the white dominions, the far Left because of the Commonwealth's neutralist, non-white majority. On some issues, certainly, the two were opposed: on the United Nations, on the independent deterrent. On other issues the two were in unexpected harmony. *Tribune* shared the pro-Russian, anti-German line over Berlin of the Beaverbrook press. (Indeed, they shared the same contributors.) Mr Michael Foot and Lord Sandwich adopted the same pro-Commonwealth, anti-Europe platform during the debate over Britain's entry to the Common Market. From both extremes of British politics, demands for British neutrality in the Cold War were heard.

What would a neutral Britain be like? There is more than one type of neutrality. And the type of neutrality desired by

Right and Left is significantly different. There is a Swedish, an Austrian, an Indian neutrality. There is a 'strong' and a 'weak' neutrality. A 'strong' neutrality is willing and able to defend itself against all comers. That was America's neutrality until 1917, and again between 1919 and 1941. Its post-war equivalent was the *troisième force*. In a different form, this is now the official policy of Gaullist France. A 'strong' neutrality requires the strongest available weapons: it requires the hydrogen bomb. With this weapon (and the means of delivery) the smallest nation state can assert its sovereignty. In any conflict that arises, it can observe an armed neutrality. That is the Gaullist conception. But it was also the conception implicit in British right-wing thinking after Suez. It was not, of course, Khrushchev's threat to bombard Britain with rockets that broke Britain at Suez. It was diplomatic isolation and American financial pressure. But it was not illogical to argue – even if one disagreed with Suez strongly, as I did – that Suez showed Britain had lost her freedom of action in certain important respects. The independent deterrent was not designed to 'duplicate' American efforts: it was intended to restore Britain's freedom of action. Perhaps the project was technically misconceived. That is another matter. But the decision to build the deterrent was a *political* decision. Even under the Attlee government the independent deterrent contained an anti-American component. If America could be fully trusted, why was a British deterrent necessary? It was on the assumption that British and American policy *might not always agree* that the Attlee government went ahead with the bomb. Was it not an unreasonable assumption? Surely, the more anti-American you are, the more reasonable it must seem. Certainly Britain showed little sign of 'neutralist' leanings at the time. The independence implied in the decision was 'strong' rather than 'weak'. The assumption was that America might one day pull out of Europe. Britain would then have to defend Europe alone against Communist aggression. That is precisely the position of de Gaulle's France today.

If the Right was tempted after Suez by the 'strong' neutralism implicit in a British independent deterrent (to Europeans, this was implicit in British abolition of conscription and reliance on massive retaliation), the Left wore its neutralism with a difference. Britain should contract out of the Cold War and adopt the non-aligned, non-nuclear, neutralist posture of the coloured Commonwealth. The motive was, originally, 'negative'. Only by leaving the Western alliance could Britain ensure her survival in nuclear war. (Of course, it is not at all certain that a 'weak' neutrality *does* ensure survival. It did not ensure Holland's or Denmark's in the last war. It is more likely that Britain, in an all-out struggle between America and Russia, would be occupied against her will. She would then have an equal chance of being destroyed by Russian bombs on American bases or American on Russian. A grisly prospect! The unilateralist calculation is wrong: destruction and dishonour are not necessarily alternatives; they could go together.) The original motive was to save British skins and consciences. But unilateralism also offered a strong positive inducement for Britain to go neutral. Britain would shake off the moral opprobrium of alignment with either of the Cold War blocs. With Nehru's India, she would become the leader of the non-aligned world. In this conception, chauvinism and neutralism were curiously blended. By adding her strength to that of the non-aligned nations, Britain would, it was argued, proportionately weaken the forces making for world war. The lesson the Right learned from Suez was that Britain's aims had been frustrated by a combination of the two nuclear super-powers. The Left saw in the frustration of Britain's Suez adventure a moral victory for 'world opinion'. Suitably strengthened, this same world opinion might be mobilized against other acts of aggression, whether Communist or Western. In the end, the Cold War might be snuffed out for lack of fuel. It was an altruistic conception. Indeed, suspiciously so. Behind it lurked a frame of mind not at all dissimilar from that on the Right. Here was a new role for Britain in the world, a role that would enhance her prestige as association with America or with Europe could not hope to. For the anti-European, anti-American Left it was an ideal solution.

Clearly, it is also a solution well calculated to appeal to a people with a diminished sense of power and large reserves of moral idealism. Consider these words of the Bishop of Coventry, as reported in the *Guardian* (13 March 1963):

The Bishop of Coventry . . . preaching in St Paul's Cathedral, said that he agreed with the recent words of Mr Dean Acheson that 'Britain had lost an empire and not yet found a role'.

Dr Bardsley said that we had lost an empire, or rather given it away, and it had been *an act of moral greatness without parallel in the history of the world* to train our daughter nations for self-government.

We stood in one of those immensely challenging and exciting times when a new and thrilling chapter in the long history of our race was about to be written. Patriotism . . . *did not depend upon outward greatness*, but would assuredly lead to real greatness. [My italics.]

It is instructive to compare this with the language anti-Europeans used about the Commonwealth during the debate on 'going into Europe'. This is what Mr William Pickles had to say in his Fabian pamphlet, *Not with Europe*:

The political objections . . . add up to an overwhelming case against British membership. The economic objections are also strong and there is in addition one other political objection which ought alone to lead us to decide against, even if none of the others existed. The E.E.C. is the wrong international grouping for Britain to join, because it is irrelevant to the principal requirements of the age we live in and destructive of *the most effective international grouping in the world today, the Commonwealth*. [My italics.]

The 'Great British' sentiment underlying both statements is apparent. How do we explain it? How do we explain the fact, so puzzling to the outsider, that enthusiasm for the Commonwealth has grown as its actual power has decreased? Certainly, the growing adulation of the Royal Family was a parallel phenomenon: the trappings of power are more popular than the reality ever was. But why should enthusiasm for the Commonwealth have ceased to be the property of the Right, and become the property of the Left?

I suggest that only the latent neutralism of the conception can explain this remarkable shift. It is to the Left that the altruistic, international, neutralist aspect of the modern Commonwealth appeals. Of course, the chauvinistic aspect is there too: *Tribune* and the *Daily Express* speak of the Commonwealth in the same tones. It is this aspect that is most evident to the outsider, as any foreign correspondent in London will tell you. To the outsider, it is obvious that the British are constructing a surrogate, fantasy empire to console themselves for the loss of the real one. That may be unkind. But it is true that in no European country are the ex-colonialists so obsessed with their colonial past. Italians, Frenchmen, Dutchmen do not continually boast of their colonial achievements. Perhaps that is because they have less to boast of – significantly, that retort would be on the tip of an Englishman's tongue. Yet the retort is unfair. The French have a great deal to their credit. Despite the horrors of Vietnam and Algeria, many consider their colonial policies to have been culturally rather more successful. Today, France gives more financial assistance to underdeveloped nations than Britain. Again, there are plenty of things in our colonial history of which we have no reason to be proud. It is arguable that Britain's concern with her Empire's successor states expresses a higher sense of responsibility. There is some truth in this; though less, as the French example shows, than is often assumed. But the fact of Britain's continuing obsession with the theme, in contrast to the rest of Europe, is not open to question.

Both in its extreme neutralist form, and as a general sentiment, the new obsession is significant. It seems to be a product of those same 'withdrawal symptoms,' that isolationism, that growing alienation from power-politics, at whose causes we have hinted. Of course, to say we exaggerate the Commonwealth's role in world affairs is not to say it has no role at all. Properly limited and defined, the Commonwealth can do the things its enthusiasts say it can. It can forge links between distant peoples, bridge distinctions of creed and colour, keep alive traditions of equity and political justice. But these are not political links in the strict sense. The links between the Nato nations, for example, are much stronger. An act of war against these islands does not commit India, Australia, or Nigeria to come to our defence. But it does commit Holland, Germany, or the United States to do so. The ties between Commonwealth countries are ties of custom, sentiment, and convenience. They vary in strength from country to country. But they are often no stronger than the ties that normally exist between independent states. The line between membership and non-membership is itself vague and arbitrary. Economically and financially, Ireland and South Africa are more intimately connected with this country than Cyprus or Canada. Yet the former are out of the Commonwealth and the latter in. This is not set down in contempt of the Commonwealth. But I submit that all arguments about what Britain might do if she 'led' the Commonwealth rest on a false premiss. The Commonwealth is not that kind of political organization. Indeed, it is not a political organization at all. The moment Britain attempted to 'lead' it, the Commonwealth would vanish into thin air.

If this conclusion is correct, it is as damaging to the neutralism of the Left as to the neo-imperialism of the Right. The opposition of the coloured Commonwealth to neo-imperialist policies can be assumed. But its unwillingness to accept Britain as the leader of a non-nuclear, non-aligned club might be no less strong. Britain is still, and will remain for many years, a colonial power. Indeed, in Central and Southern Africa, she is approaching the most difficult years of her colonial history – at a moment when the process of decolonialization is complete in the case of every Euro-

pean power except Portugal. On the Persian gulf, Britain
has vitally important interests, whose ultimate sanction is
armed force. The future of Malaysia is unsettled. Yet even
were Britain to shed *all* her dependencies, she would remain
'colonialist' in the eyes of Afro-Asians. It is not only the past
they remember. They argue that Britain's interests, like
those of France and Germany, are those of an advanced
European industrial power. Nor are they wrong. The strongest argument against Britain's joining a non-nuclear, non-
aligned club is that she would be blackballed by its present
members. There is a further difficulty. Britain is said to lack
'national purpose'. The far Left sees a national purpose for
Britain in giving the new nations the benefit of our advice
and experience. It is a noble aim. But it conceals a contradiction. It is true that the new nations look to us for guidance. But this means that Britain must herself be strong and
self-confident: she can hardly seek guidance from those who
seek it from her. Few poetic commands have been as fiercely
ridiculed as Kipling's 'Take up the White Man's Burden!'.
Today, the command takes a different form. As the guilty
conscience of white Europe, the White Man's Burden is still
with us, and nowhere more so than in Britain. I do not dispute that we should bear this burden: I believe we should
give more aid than we do. I dispute only that, as former imperialists, we can rid ourselves of the burden by creeping
into other men's skins.

The illusions of the Right are often more straightforward, and therefore more vulnerable, than those of the
Left. It was no accident that, during the Common Market–
Commonwealth debate of 1961–2, the realists about the
Commonwealth were to be found on the Right, the senti-
mentalists on the Left. The reversal of position was remarkable, but not surprising. The Right has its own sentimen-
talities, but it does not lack a sense of power. The Right's
crucial argument was that Europe's power was rising and
that of the Commonwealth declining. General de Gaulle's
rebuff in no way affects the truth of this perception. Indeed,

the rising power of Europe is a further argument against British neutralism. It is arguable that, if the British people accepted neutralism, they would be willing to accept its consequences. But those who advocate neutralism are not frank about its consequences. A neutral Britain would obviously not be acceptable to the Common Market – less so than Sweden, Austria, and Switzerland, who can plead mitigating circumstances. America, the largest foreign investor in Britain, would quickly divert the mainstream of her investment to Common Market Europe. Concerning Europe's security and political future Britain would no longer be consulted, by either Europe or America. Having abandoned the Western alliance, Britain could not expect American support in those parts of the world where it is still vital to her. This, too, might have serious political and economic consequences. It is not necessary to stress the effects on British home politics: mass unemployment, a declining standard of living, a permanent sense of insecurity and inferiority could give rise to something far more frightening than the malaise of the past decade. Nor is it so certain we should be left alone 'to stew in our own juice'. Our condition might come to warrant foreign intervention. Do the neutralists ever consider these possibilities? I, for one, believe a neutral Britain would not be a Britain worth living in.

Fortunately, it is a vision unlikely to be realized. But the neutralist tendencies are there. Few people would go all the way with the neutralism of C.N.D. But many would assent to the crypto-neutralist sentiment implied in the wish that 'Britain ought to mediate between Russia and America'. The sentiment is crypto-neutralist for this reason. One cannot claim to have a 'special relationship' with America and also claim to be the impartial judge of her actions. The role of honest broker is not open to the country that would be America's staunchest ally. This is not to say that Britain should not criticize America. But we ought to recognize the hidden neutralism in these arguments. If it is not apparent to us, it is certainly apparent to our friends. It is also apparent to our enemies. I believe it lies behind that attitude to the Cold War which has come to seem specifically British.

On the Continent, post-war tendencies towards neutralism – in the 'weak', not the 'strong' sense – have been dramatically reversed. Like American isolationism, they seemed to have passed into British political consciousness. And if Britain and Europe, like Britain and America, have exchanged roles, the explanation is to be found in the political experiences of Britain and Europe since 1940. I have argued that Europe had to learn by violence certain lessons which, however unpleasant at the time, were to prove salutary in the long run. By violence, Europeans learnt what foreign conquest and occupation by a totalitarian enemy implies. By violence, Europeans learnt what Communism means in practice. By violence, Europeans learnt what it means to lose an empire. I do not say this in praise of violence. But I believe Germany and France, Italy, Belgium, and Holland learnt something which Britain, in her very gentleness, failed to learn. They learnt not only that loss of empire is an irreversible and agonizing process, but that it necessitates a total national reorientation. Nostalgia for empire, powerful in Britain, has almost vanished from the continent of Europe. In the end, the loss of empire has hurt us more. That it should be so is cruelly ironic. Our post-war record in liberating our dependent territories was better than that of our neighbours. What our eulogists say of the benefits Britain's ex-colonies have reaped from their experience with Britain is all true. What they fail to mention is the damage this gentle passing of empire has done to Britain.

III. Britain and the Totalitarians

CHAPTER 6

IN THE THIRTIES

(i) Hitler

ONE'S country, like one's self, is unique. At least, it is flattering to think so. How quaint, how complex, how contrary we are! How baffling to the rational foreign eye! So, in an inhospitable, unmannerly world, we shrink from comprehension. Let the barbarians breed like rabbits, let them perform prodigious mechanical feats: at least they will never understand us. Not understanding us, they will retire, or risk ingestion: that is how India dealt with all her conquerors, and finally with ourselves. And Britain? Having lost the supremacy, must she settle for mediocrity? Will she turn in on herself, seeking comfort in nostalgia? Or will she resort to barbarian methods to win barbarian respect? Britain may be unique, but her situation is not. France, Spain, Germany gained the supremacy and lost it. Portugal, Holland, Austria, and Sweden gained empires and lost them. What was their response? Portugal froze, France smouldered, Holland grew rich, Germany went mad, Austria forgot, Spain was too proud to notice; Europe is a showcase of variants. Whose way will Britain go? Not Germany's; not Holland's; not Austria's. Will she smoulder like France, perhaps; freeze like Portugal; or, like Spain, be too proud to notice?

The temptation is to stop the clock. The temptation, for the country that has been first-rate, is to become anything but second-rate. Better, by far, to be nothing! That seems to have been Portugal's choice. The growth of neutralism suggests that Britain too has been tempted that way. Yet the fallacy is plain: stopping one's clock does not stop the neighbours' clocks. If history is indeed over for Portugal (which remains to be seen), Portugal owes that to geography. Spain, scarcely less isolated, found herself involved in Europe's civil war. France after the First World War and Germany after the Second would have liked to retire from the game. Economics, geography, politics forbade it. What fed European neutralism after 1945, and feeds British neutralism now, is the desire for a holiday from history, the wish to retire into a corner and lick one's wounds. If the Cold War had not come about, Europe might have done just this. If neutralism has grown in Britain, it is because we are shielded from the impact of the Cold War, as Europe is not. The temptation to stop the clock is stronger, because the neighbours' clocks are faint. Or is the converse true? Do the neighbours' clocks seem faint only because the wish to stop our own is so strong?

The story of the impact of Nazi and Communist totalitarianism on Britain suggests the latter is more nearly true. About the appeasement policy of the thirties there is now little room for dispute. Hitler demolished its premises so completely that it has few posthumous defenders. The most that can be said is that Chamberlain, Halifax, Dawson, and the rest were men of good will. But even that was evident at the time. Why did a British government, with the support of the British people, base its policy on these premises? Why was opposition to that policy ineffective? If recent British policy, as I believe, has been based on similar false premises, is it unreasonable to assume kinship of motive? Once again, there is no question of malevolent intent. Those English liberals who propose the same policy towards Russia Britain once pursued towards Germany are men of good will. Indeed, it is the spirit of good will that leads them to these premises. That does not, of course, make the premises any less mistaken. But it makes it important to examine the kinship of motive.

Perhaps the question should be turned about: who opposed appeasement, and why? The answer is more astonishing than is usually allowed. The two groups who most resolutely rejected appeasement were the intellectuals of the Left and the friends of Winston Churchill. No two groups could have been more unlike. What was revealed to these men that was hidden from their fellow-citizens? What did they have in common that gave them superior insight? The answer, I believe, is that both were radically out of sympathy with the Britain of the thirties. It was their rejection of the complacent assumptions of the age of Baldwin, MacDonald, and Chamberlain that set them apart. If the intellectuals of the Left understood the significance of Nazism, they owed this to their unpopular socialist principles. Struggling against reaction and obscurantism in Britain, they understood very well what Nazism was about. Among intellectuals, the traditions of socialist internationalism were still alive. The first refugees from Nazi Germany and Fascist Italy were people like themselves. They brought with them a vivid estimate of the methods and intentions of Fascism. Ideology and experience combined to make intellectuals aware of the dangers approaching Britain. The policies they proposed to deal with these dangers were not always realistic. Even when they were, they were often vitiated by the pacifism of the older left-wing tradition. (It is true that the same factors that alerted the Left to the meaning of Nazism blinded it to the meaning of Communism. We shall return to this point.) Again, the influence of the left-wing intelligentsia was limited. But it should not be underestimated. We have only to think of what Churchill would have achieved, if in addition to his unpopularity with his own party, he had remained 'Churchill the warmonger' to the English Left.

It is Churchill's understanding of the Nazi menace that sheds most light on the mentality of those who failed to understand it. Comparison between the roles played by Halifax and Churchill in the thirties is instructive. If the Nazis had never existed, and we were to judge the two men by their imperial policies, there is not much doubt what our judgement would be. Halifax, as Viceroy at New Delhi in the early thirties, was the first great practitioner of that policy towards colonial peoples of which, thirty years later, most Englishmen are proud. It would not be wrong to call that policy appeasement, if the word itself had not its very special and distasteful meaning. The policy Britain then adopted towards her Empire was certainly, as Churchill insisted, a strategy of retreat. To most of us, a generation later, this must seem the only wise and realistic strategy. But to Churchill the very notion of retreat was repugnant. It is easy to dismiss this as a great man's blind spot, a piece of unregenerate, emotional Blimpism. But that does small justice to Churchill's intelligence. Churchill's apprehensions were rational enough. He feared that any relaxation of the imperial will-to-power might lead to a general weakening, and encourage Britain's enemies in their hostile intents. Perhaps Churchill was wrong. Perhaps a quicker transfer of power would have strengthened British India when Japan attacked in December 1941. But it is possible to argue *both* that Halifax's Indian policies were just *and* that these signs of a weakening of British power encouraged German Nazis and Japanese militarism.

Within five years Halifax and Churchill were again bitterly opposed. I am not arguing that Halifax applied his Indian experiences to the problem of Nazi Germany. But the same kind of issue now divided Churchill and Halifax as had divided them over India. Over India, it seems to us, Churchill was wrong: appeasement was the correct policy. Why was this? The premise of appeasement is that political movements have a saturation point. Once that point is reached, the danger is removed. It follows that it is reasonable to make all concessions up to that point. The saturation point of Indian nationalism in the thirties lay well this side of complete independence. India could have acquired self-governing status within a Commonwealth rather more tightly knit than that of today. If that was the Indian aim, it was reasonable to make concessions. But the same was not true of Germany and Japan. To Churchill, these were expanding imperialist powers whose appetite would grow with every triumph. That appears self-evident to us today. But to most Englishmen in the thirties it was not. Why were they blind to the danger? Plainly, they judged others by themselves. A satisfied power, Britain was no longer familiar with the mentality of nations in their lusty imperialist youth. Churchill, who had fought in India, the Sudan, and South Africa in his youth, knew how empires are built. His intimates were not the comfortable businessmen, the well-spoken public-schoolboys, who ran Britain after the fall of Lloyd George. They were men like himself: buccaneers and empire-builders of a different stamp: Beaverbrook, Smuts, Lindemann, Bracken, Birkenhead. These men were a survival from the heroic age of British imperialism, an age of which their fellow-countrymen were now ashamed. But the same qualities that made these men imperialists enabled them to understand Hitler where their fellow-countrymen failed.

Looking back, we speak of the 'Men of Munich'. That is a convenient fiction. It was not the British people who were to blame, but Chamberlain, Halifax, Dawson, Simon, Nevile Henderson. It is true that, strictly speaking, the government of the day had no mandate for appeasement. But at the general election of 1935 Baldwin, impressed by the success of the Peace Ballot, had pledged the British government to 'collective security' and to support of the League of Nations. The Peace Ballot, like most documents of its kind, was ambiguous. The public was asked five questions:

1. Should Great Britain remain a member of the League of Nations?

2. Are you in favour of an all-round reduction by agreement of international armaments?

3. Are you in favour of the all-round abolition of national military and naval aircraft by international agreement?

4. Should the manufacture and sale of armaments for private profit be prohibited by international agreement?

5. Do you consider that, if a nation insists on attacking another, the other nations should combine to compel it to stop

(a) by economic and non-military measures?

(b) if necessary, by military measures?

The first four questions expected, and received, an affirmative reply: ten million 'yeses' to an odd hundred thousand 'noes'. But the sting was in the tail: 'if necessary, military measures'. Whereas ten millions had been prepared to vote for 'economic and non-military measures', the support for military sanctions dropped to under half that figure: two and a half million people rejected military sanctions altogether.

No doubt polls of this kind mean very little. But the Peace Ballot does seem to have expressed, in its very confusion, the mood of the British public in the thirties. The general sentiment was for peace and reduction of armaments. Five, ten years earlier this sentiment – and the desire to conciliate Germany that went with it – would have been farsighted and constructive. But now it was too late. Only a very rapid increase in British armaments could preserve peace in Europe. By 1935 it was plain that Germany had begun to re-arm. A generation earlier, the British public would not have responded to German and Japanese ambitions with the same complacency. Now public indifference seemed unshakeable. It may be said that the Peace Ballot was not a programme for a self-respecting government. But at least the government which proceeded to operate in its spirit cannot be accused of acting contrary to the people's will. In trying to buy Germany off with concessions, rather than meeting her with equal force, the Men of Munich were doing what the people wanted.

(ii) Stalin

In France the failure to resist Nazism was a failure of nerve. In Britain it was a failure of the understanding. On the Continent the new total state was sufficiently like the police states of the past, with their controlled press, their pogroms, and their police brutality, to be seen for what it was. In Britain the significance of the new total state in Russia and Germany was not understood. It is evident that Churchill himself did not see its significance. Churchill's instincts told him only that Germany's new will-to-power was a threat to Britain. He remarked that, should she ever fall into Germany's condition, he would hope for a Hitler to restore Britain to her place among the nations. The remark shows two things: Churchill's grasp of the new national mood which Hitler had exploited in Germany, and his relative incomprehension of the new state the Nazis were building. It was the Left, with its international affiliations and its distrust of authority, which had the deeper understanding of what Hitler was about. In the event, neither Churchill's rhetoric, nor the shrill warnings of the Left, could avert the Munich disaster. Perhaps only at Dunkirk was the real meaning of Hitler's New Order brought home to the people of Britain. But the years of Left Book Club propaganda had played their part in the education of Britain.

Yet it was in those same years, when the truth about Nazism was emerging, that the foundations were laid for the tragic misunderstanding of another totalitarianism. The British people's lack of understanding for Nazi totalitarianism is easy to forgive: it was something quite beyond their experience. But the charge against those intellectuals who condoned in the case of Russia what they vociferously condemned in the case of Germany is graver. It is easy to make fun of the intellectual follies of the thirties. I would not re-open the question if I did not think it had some bearing in our present troubles. I am not, in comparing the two reactions, equating Nazism and communism. In applying to both the term 'totalitarian' I am only assenting to the view that they share a common structure. Whether they share common aims is another matter. I would go some way with the view that Communism has a theoretical humanistic core which Nazism lacks. But an abstract approach does not get us very far. In practice, Communist regimes have shown themselves capable of cruelties equal to those of Nazism. Comparisons involving degrees of human suffering are invidious. But the number of human beings done to death in Russia and China by direct political action (excluding war) exceeds the number done to death by the Nazis by many millions. I am not arguing that communism is 'better' or 'worse' than Nazism – only that their human destructiveness is comparable. But, it may be objected, has not communism, since Stalin's day, turned over a new leaf? Is not Khrushchev's Russia – if not Mao's China – a very different place? Has not communism undergone, in short, a process of 'liberalization'?

It is a vital question. Indeed, it is the question at the core of this book. Here, for example, is what Bertrand Russell has to say of it in his Penguin Special *Unarmed Victory* (1963):

We are told, and many of us believe, that non-Communists stand for freedom, while Communist governments impose a kind of slavery. I will admit at once that there is not as much freedom in Communist countries as I should wish to see. But I must add that the same is true of the anti-Communist countries. It might be enlightening to compare the cases of Ivinskaya in Russia and Morton Sobell in the U.S. . . . In America, communism has recently become a crime. *Throughout the years since Stalin's death, there has been increasing freedom in the East and diminishing freedom in the West, with the result that, by this time, the difference is not very notable.* Meanwhile, hatred and readiness for war are inculcated in the West and in China and India, but no longer in Russia. [My italics.]

The importance of this argument is evident. For if liberalization has indeed taken place, certain assumptions about communism on which the West has acted in the past may now be invalid. Britain, accused of being 'soft on communism' by her allies, may have arrived at a correcter estimate of Communist intentions; the theory of liberalization, in fact, is the rationale of the British view of the Cold War. On the other hand, if no significant liberalization has taken place, or if, as I believe, its significance for the external policies of the Soviet Union has been misunderstood, then the validity of the British view of the Cold War is challenged. But to look at recent British assumptions in perspective, it is important to see what assumptions have been made about communism by British intellectuals in the past, and why. If past assumptions have proved false, it may be that present assumptions should be re-examined. I make no apology, therefore, for taking a fresh look at the errors British intellectuals made about Soviet communism a generation ago.

What was it, for instance, that caused G. D. H. Cole to declare he would rather 'be ruled by Stalin than by a pack of half-witted and half-hearted Social Democrats' (*Europe, Russia, and the Future*, 1942)? Does wartime sympathy for Russia alone explain this sentiment? Earlier, he had admitted suppressions of liberty, but had argued:

Great suppression of personal liberties was unavoidable if the new order were to survive at all. Already, I believe, the Soviet Union is feeling its way towards the restoration of many of those liberties which had to be curtailed. . . . We shall find they are not merely putting back the liberties they have restricted, but establishing a new and higher kind of liberty, hitherto unknown in the world – a liberty extending to every section of the people, and women equally with men. Let us not forget that many of us – especially those who are comfortable British bourgeois – are inclined to think of liberty mainly in terms of the forms of freedom which we actually enjoy as a class privilege, and to ignore altogether those basic liberties of human life which the great majority of people have never yet possessed in any country of the world.

The date of this passage is 1937 (from the *Proceedings of the Second National Congress of Peace and Friendship with the U.S.S.R.*). Yet that year saw the climax of the Great Purge, a holocaust bloodier than anything Hitler had yet staged. We know now that some three millions lost their lives in the purge. True, the extent of the killings was difficult to estimate then. Few intellectuals knew Russia well, and the censorship was rigid. But the Moscow trials certainly did not lack publicity. Their clumsy fabrications, now officially admitted in the U.S.S.R., were apparent to many non-professional observers. Yet the celebrated liberal journalist A. J. Cummings could write (*News Chronicle*, 25 August 1936):

> The evidence and the confessions are so circumstantial that to reject both as hocus-pocus would be to reduce the trial almost to complete unintelligibility.

Sir Bernard Pares, a well-known expert on Russian affairs, also attended the trials. He wrote (*Spectator*, 18 September 1936):

> I have made a careful study of the verbatim report. I must give it as my considered judgement that if the report had been issued in a country [that is, other than the U.S.S.R.] without any of the antecedents I have referred to, the trial would be regarded as one which could not fail to carry conviction. . . . The examination of the sixteen accused by the State Prosecutor is a close work of dispassionate reasoning in which, in spite of some denials and more evasions, the guilt of the accused is completely brought home.

In the same year, the Moscow correspondent of the *New Statesman* was writing:

> The new Soviet Constitution is not merely a promise. Many of its provisions register changes which have already taken place . . . the slow eclipse of the G.P.U. commenced in 1931. . . . Ruthlessness and terror had ceased to be the state's most trusted weapons. . . . The reign of law is now definitely established in the U.S.S.R. There is little doubt that if the present normal times continue – in other words, if there is no foreign war – Soviet citizens will hereafter enjoy inviolability of person, home, and mail. . . . Dictatorship yields to democracy.

The passage repays careful study. Here, at the very climax of the Terror ('the present normal times . . .'), the talk was also of 'liberalization'. The conclusion is inescapable: what the reader is being offered here is not factual reporting, it is the projection of a wish-dream. A correspondent in the *New Statesman* (Pearl Binder, 7 March 1936) gives these impressions of life in Russia:

> It is collectivization which has finally conquered the food problem; the bounteous results cram the food shops of the entire Soviet

Union – delegations of peasants from the Ukraine, Uzbekistan from all the national minorities, come to Moscow to tell how much better off they are than before. . . .

From Khrushchev's own statements we know that this account was not so much exaggerated as exactly contrary to the facts. The collectivization campaign of the early thirties, in the course of which some three million people were deported and tens of millions expropriated (the ensuing famine alone killed three millions), set back Soviet agriculture for a generation. It was a disaster from which Russia is only now beginning to recover. Yet it was almost universally believed in the thirties and forties – and not only in fellow-travelling circles – that collectivization had indeed 'conquered the food problem'.

The most extreme and most famous aberration was that of the Webbs. *Soviet Communism: A New Civilization?* is a dead horse by now. Nevertheless, I ask the reader's indulgence to flog it once more. For the kind of error the Webbs fell into about Soviet Russia tells us a good deal about the attitudes of other commentators at the time. The case of the Webbs, after all, is very extraordinary. If the Webbs were famous in sociological, political, and economic research, it was for their painstaking empiricism. It was their intellectual influence that had prevented Marxism from getting the hold on the English left-wing intelligentsia it enjoyed in Europe. It is true that they were 'bureaucratically minded' and might not find Stalin's methods, and his contempt for the masses, as uncongenial as more libertarian English socialists. But the Webbs were trained social observers, with much practical experience of government and party organization. They were not fellow-travellers with a *Schwärmerei* for Soviet Russia. Indeed, no one despised the fellow-travelling socialist more than they. Yet they could write (p. xxi):

It is clear that, tested by the Constitution of the Soviet Union as revised and enacted in 1936, the U.S.S.R. is the most inclusive and equalized democracy in the world.

There is irony in the phrase 'tested by . . .'. From what follows it is clear that this written Constitution was their main source of knowledge. Here, for instance, is what they had to say about Stalin (p. 332), as the climax of his personal Terror approached:

Sometimes it is asserted that, whereas the form may be otherwise, the fact is that while the Communist Party controls the whole administration, the Party itself, and thus indirectly the whole state, is governed by the will of a single person, Josef Stalin. First let it be noted that, unlike Mussolini, Hitler, and other modern dictators, Stalin is not invested by law with any authority over his fellow-citizens, and not even over the members of the Party to which he belongs.

Of the 'personality cult', later to be condemned by Khrushchev, the Webbs had this to say (p. xlv):

Among the leaders of the Communist Party there ensued a tacit understanding that Stalin should be 'boosted' as the supreme leader of the proletariat, the Party, and the state. His portrait and his bust were accordingly distributed by tens of thousands. But the idolization of Stalin has largely ceased to exist in the Soviet Union today. Moreover, Stalin's recent step down from the pedestal of the Holy Father of the Communist Party to the prosaic position of Prime Minister, elected strictly according to the constitutional procedure of a political democracy, has, so to speak, secularized his status and made it that of any other Prime Minister ultimately dependent on the votes of the people.

On the role of the G.P.U. in the middle thirties, they commented (p. 487):

. . . there is now, we think, little or no sign of general disapproval among the four-fifths of the people who are manual workers in industry or agriculture, either of its continued existence or of its vigorous activities. . . . 'In all fairness,' writes the one who has put into a book the most personal knowledge of the G.P.U., 'I must add that, wherever the G.P.U. strikes, it is usually with reason. Perhaps the accusation is trumped up or exaggerated; perhaps the particular incident leading to the arrest is but a pretext. Yet behind these possibly flimsy excuses, the G.P.U. is practically dead certain

the accused was engaged in activities against the state. When they
do strike, they strike sure and hard. Their case is practically water-
tight.'

On the issue of free speech, like many lesser commentators,
they tried to turn the tables on the critic of the U.S.S.R.
(p. xiv):

It is not surprising therefore that [threatened with foreign
invasion] there should have been intolerance on the part of the
Soviet government towards free thought and expression, by word
and by writ, of antagonism to its home and foreign policy. How
does this intolerance differ in character from the intolerance mani-
fested in Great Britain? As we have already described, free
criticism, however hostile it may be, is permitted, even encouraged,
in the U.S.S.R. . . . Moreover, when anxious to encourage
historical research the Soviet government is singularly open-
minded . . .

One point should be noted. None of these witnesses can be
described, to the best of my knowledge, as a 'fellow-traveller'. It would be easy to select similar quotations from the
writings of known Communists or fellow-travellers. But that
is a different matter; a matter of honest stupidity or conscious
deceit. In the writings we have considered the *sincerity*
of the observer is not in question. Some other explanation
must be found. With the Webbs, I believe, the key lay
in their continuing reverence for a document, even when
that document was a fabrication. As A. J. Cummings said,
the documentation of the trials was so circumstantial that 'to
reject it as hocus pocus would reduce the trial almost to
complete unintelligibility'. The assumption of these English
observers was that the evidence, though a little strained,
could not be *wholly* false. If it were, doubt would be cast on
the credibility of *all* official information about the Soviet
Union. Any foreign correspondent is trained to a certain
scepticism in these matters. But the idea of a state falsifying
the whole range of the information it supplies, not only to
foreigners but to its own citizens, went beyond British

experience or imagination at the time. It is arguable that, with the evidence of Goebbels's press and the van der Lubbe trial before them, British intellectuals ought to have been on their guard. But the wish to believe in the potential goodness of the Soviet system – indeed, to believe in it as the answer to Nazism – was too strong to allow of any such comparison. If there had been crimes, they were in the past; a 'slow eclipse of the G.P.U.' was to be expected; 'liberalization' was written in the stars; in a little while, a 'new and higher kind of liberty' would be ushered in.

Why did the British Left, which quickly saw the meaning of Nazi totalitarianism, fail to see the identical symptoms in Soviet Russia? Certainly, there were honourable exceptions: George Orwell, and Bertrand Russell himself, whose *Theory and Practice of Bolshevism*, written in 1921, proved uncannily prescient about Stalin. Clearly, there was a strong element of wish-fulfilment in the British Left's view of Russia. The reason is evident. After Labour's defeat in 1931, British socialists, G. D. H. Cole and the Webbs among them, were deeply pessimistic about the future of socialism in Britain. Russia was the guarantee that socialism did, after all, work. These British apologists did not set up Soviet Russia as a model. They did not want communism in Britain. If they wanted it in Russia, that had something to do with Russia being far away. Motives were mixed. There was a belief that Stalin's ruthlessness would strengthen Russia for the coming struggle with Germany. This patriotic and perhaps realistic argument (though it is a moot point whether Stalin's ruthlessness strengthened the Soviet state more than it weakened it) was in plain contradiction to the libertarian claims made for Russia. But it was present in many Englishmen's minds. Add, too, the contempt for foreigners evident in this easy tolerance of what the liberal Englishman would certainly have condemned at home.

There is a further reason for the mistakes that were made, one that has not lost its relevance today. Could the assertions about the Soviet Union we have quoted have been made by intelligent liberal Englishmen about any other foreign country? Could a British left-winger have said of the United States during the New Deal that it was 'establishing a new and higher kind of liberty, hitherto unknown in the world'? Of the examination of Sacco and Vanzetti that it was 'a close work of dispassionate reasoning in which the guilt of the accused is completely brought home'? Of Roosevelt's agricultural policy that it had 'finally solved the food problem: the bounteous results cram the food shops'? Evidently not. Yet these statements would have been truer of the United States than they ever were of the Soviet Union. The reason for the difference is plain. The terminology employed to describe Soviet reality is, with slight modifications, the terminology employed by the Communists themselves. How did Soviet Communists, so ignorant of the ways of the West and so contemptuous of Western liberal intellectuals, succeed in establishing this intellectual control?

It is not clear how far the Russian Communists ever deliberately set out to influence Western intellectuals. The Moscow trials were meant for home consumption; that Western liberals believed in them was a happy by-product. The explanation is perhaps simpler. The policies of total secrecy and of the big lie, intended to serve a humbler purpose, proved a useful complement to Western liberal utopianism. Because nothing was really known, the foreigner was grateful for the smallest scrap of information. Because nothing could be checked, the statement that 'three million people had been killed by collectivization' was as much or as little to be believed as the official statistics. Since few people could bring themselves to believe in the *total* mendacity of the Soviet system, some proportion of what the government said would always be believed. Among those who, for one reason or another, wished the Soviet experiment well, a large proportion would be believed. In face of Soviet reality, the intellectual tests which the Webbs would have insisted upon elsewhere were abandoned. Perhaps, in their hearts, the Webbs knew that there were no facts to go on.

Rather than admit this, with all that it implied about the Soviet Union, they accepted Soviet intellectual control. The result was a work as turgid and mendacious as the Soviet Constitution itself. There is no more extraordinary case of *trahison des clercs* in English intellectual history.

CHAPTER 7

IN THE SIXTIES

(i) *The Logic of Appeasement*

THE temptation is to stop the clock. How else do we explain the British people's mistake about Hitler, a mistake they would not have made fifty years before? How else do we explain the resistance to Munich by such contradictory groupings – by resolute imperialists on the one hand, and by resolute anti-imperialists on the other? How else but by assuming that the imperialism of the English middle classes had become by the thirties a satisfied, conservative, scrupulous imperialism, forgetful of its own less scrupulous origins? Needless to say, I do not equate moral scrupulousness with decadence. But there is a connexion – in history, if not in logic – between the welcome growth of scruple and the weakened sense of power. Years of anti-imperialist propaganda, admirable in its motives, had undermined the good conscience of the English middle class. Imperial will-to-power had become transmuted into good stewardship. The notion of the White Man's Burden, once the robust expression of moral superiority, was now charged with a sense of guilt. It was a victory for sweetness and light. But it led to a new hypocrisy. The violence underlying every political order, including the British Empire of the thirties, was conveniently forgotten. The British people, still conscious of the power they held, but acquiescent in its eventual devolution, began to believe that no problems existed that could not be settled by conciliation, negotiation, and compromise. Both Churchill the imperialist and the anti-imperialists of the Left knew this was not so. They knew Hitler could not be stopped in this way. Their motives could not have been more different. But they both knew, with Mao Tse-tung, that 'political success grows out of the barrel of a gun'. The British people had put this truism out of mind.

Dunkirk, it is said, changed all that. Whatever unrealism Britain displayed in the thirties, the British people made up for it by their stand against Hitler. Never again would a British government be allowed to pursue a policy of appeasement. That is the official version. It is flattering enough. It admits the stain of Munich. But it argues that it was wiped out by the Battle of Britain and Alamein. Britain has purged herself. Let foreigners divert their attention from her hour of shame to her hour of glory. But what do foreigners think, in fact? I suggest that, while honouring Britain for her stand in 1940, they think less flatteringly of Britain's posture now. Earlier, I quoted from Mr Joseph Fromm's report on Cuba Week:

The British believe in compromise. It was this spirit Hitler exploited at Munich. During the Cuba crisis, it appeared that many of Britain's most influential people have yet to learn the lesson of Munich.

Americans are too polite; they do not usually tell the British what they think of them. But Mr Fromm is not alone in thinking that the Britain of today is closer to the Britain of Munich than to the Britain of Dunkirk. We may disagree with this judgement. But it is not masochistic to try to see ourselves as others see us. When Mr Acheson said in his West Point speech that Britain 'had pursued a policy as weak as its military capacity' we should realize that – despite diplomatic denials – he expressed a general sentiment. Again, it was not polite of Dr Adenauer to remark to British journalists that 'an urge to join Europe is not compatible with appeasement of Russia'. But he was only saying what the majority of Germans felt during the Berlin crisis. Doubtless he echoed also the opinion of General de Gaulle. In the euphoria of Mr Macmillan's trip to Moscow, it was overlooked that Britain's popularity had decreased in France and Germany as rapidly as Mr Macmillan's had increased in Britain. No doubt General de Gaulle has reasons for disliking us of which the reason knows nothing. But many Europeans and many Americans would not think his distrust of Britain's 'weak policy' in the Cold War irrational. It is exaggerating only a little to say that Mr Macmillan's trip to Moscow cost him his trip to Brussels.

Appeasement is a rude word. But the word can be defined, and its emotional charge reduced. In essence, appeasement is neither good nor bad; it is merely one policy among others. Appeasement is a policy of calculated concession. Depending on the circumstances, such a policy may be appropriate or inappropriate. But the circumstances go beyond the immediate tactical strength or weakness of the enemy. The enemy's intentions are a part of the circumstances. If the British had been determined to stay in India, appeasement of Indian nationalism would have been inappropriate. Stern repression would have been more rational. Equally, if Indian nationalism had threatened to expropriate British business, massacre British women and children, and turn the clock back to the dark ages, stern repression would have been rational – indeed, on the analogy of the Mau Mau rising, it would have been right. But these extremes did not express the intentions of either British imperialism or Indian nationalism. Beneath the disagreement there was a core of common interest. Once that core had been reached, compromise would be possible. From the beginning, this was well known to the protagonists. 'Appeasement' was therefore an appropriate policy for Britain to adopt towards Indian nationalism.

Towards German nationalism, under Adolf Hitler, it was inappropriate. Or so it seems to us now. Yet, to give the Men of Munich their due, appeasement of Germany was rational on their own assumptions. Nor were these assumptions so ill-founded. From *Mein Kampf* onwards, Hitler had aimed to preserve the 'integrity of the British Empire'. This followed from his general belief in Nordic hegemony. Let the Germans rule the Eurasian heartland; the British their maritime Empire. The appeasers were not wholly wrong; a theoretical point did exist at which a compromise with Hitler was possible. Unfortunately, as Churchill saw, that point lay beyond Britain's traditional margin of safety. It would have meant German domination of the Continent 'from Brest to the Urals'. Britain could keep her Empire. Indeed, she might hold it more securely. But Britain's own freedom would depend on Nazi tolerance. That possibility was presented to the British people after Dunkirk. But they were now agreed in finding it unacceptable. Britain could still have made her peace with Hitler. But the British people now shared Churchill's view that appeasement could only be achieved at an unacceptable price.

It is clear that the same argument can be applied to Russian and Chinese communism. The 'appeasement' of communism is appropriate if a point of compromise exists within the margin of safety. On the face of it, this would seem a doubtful assumption. Marxism–Leninism is a universalist doctrine. It makes two fundamental assertions about the world we live in: one 'scientific', one 'moral'. It asserts that ineluctable historical and economic forces are transforming the system it calls capitalism into the system it calls socialism. It asserts equally that this transformation represents a moral advance so great that the individual ought to devote his life to bringing it about. It is not clear in what relation these assertions stand to one another; they might even appear to be contradictory. Nevertheless, to assert the one has been, with Marx as with Lenin, to assert the other. It follows that coexistence is ideologically impossible between communism and capitalism. This Mr Khrushchev has frequently confirmed. Whether it follows that coexistence between capitalist and Communist states is impossible, except as an armed truce, is more debatable. The sting of the original doctrine can be drawn by abandoning the corollary that war between the two systems is inevitable. But to say

that Marxism–Leninism can tolerate the existence of capitalism, in any but a tactical sense, is to contradict its two
fundamental assertions. Western optimists and Chinese dog-
matists maintain that Khrushchev is doing just this.

I agree to this extent: Marxist–Leninist dogma has never
been the sole determinant of Soviet or Chinese foreign policy. If it had been, the Soviet Union would have followed
Trotsky's policy of revolution, not Stalin's policy of 'socialism in one country'. Nevertheless, to dismiss Marxism–
Leninism from the reckoning would be hasty. It would be
rash to argue that once-militant Marxism–Leninism, like
Islam and Christendom before it, had passed into a 'quiescent phase'. In any case, how do we decide? How do we
assess degrees of ideological militancy? All we can assess is
the practical militancy of Communist behaviour. I shall try
to do this by examining specific cases in the following chapters. Yet we cannot avoid speculation altogether. For the
optimist's assumption that a point of compromise exists, and
is acceptable, rests on a double speculation: that Marxism–
Leninism is not to be taken literally, and that traditional
Russian and Chinese ambitions, which have taken the place
of the doctrine, are limited. The optimist may be right; but
his assumptions are speculative. The pessimist's fear that
Marxism–Leninism and traditional national ambitions may
reinforce one another is also speculative. Yet there can be no
intelligent foreign policy without an estimate of Soviet Communist and Chinese Communist intentions. How do we
escape from the dilemma?

Tactically, we can analyse specific Communist policies as
they have evolved since Stalin's death. We can see whether
the methods have altered. But strategically? To many, Communist intentions are a mystery wrapped in an enigma. But
surely the burden of proof falls on those who *deny* that
Marxism–Leninism means what it says? About Stalin's
Russia, there is no disagreement. But Russia is still ruled by
Stalin's heirs, through Stalin's party. If Russia has grown
more liberal, the burden of proof is on those who assert this.

I shall try to present the arguments of the protagonists of liberalization as fairly as possible. But I shall differ with their conclusions. There is, of course, much common ground. Nobody denies that there have been improvements in the Soviet Union since Stalin's death. Equally, nobody in the West can be other than delighted at this. But on the conclusions to be drawn – particularly on the conclusions for our foreign policy – there will be considerable disagreement. What sections of Soviet society does liberalization affect, and in what ways? Does liberalization go hand in hand with the growth of education and the rise in the standard of living? Are nations with a high standard of living and education always less aggressive than other nations? Does internal liberalization, however we may define it, necessarily influence a state's external behaviour? Might not a more confident, less aggressive policy at home be consistent with a more confident, more aggressive policy abroad? We shall take up these arguments later. Let us first hear what the protagonists of liberalization have to say.

(ii) Khrushchev

The two best-known exponents of the liberalization hypothesis are Mr Edward Crankshaw and Mr Isaac Deutscher. Both have extensive knowledge of the Soviet Union. Both have been professional commentators on Soviet affairs since the nineteen-forties. Mr Deutscher was born in Poland and had first-hand experience of communism, and in particular of the Trotsky–Stalin struggle, in Eastern Europe in the thirties. Mr Crankshaw spent much of the Second World War in Russia. Since the war, he has written regularly for the *Observer* on all aspects of Soviet life, revisiting Russia several times since Stalin's death. Both present the liberalization hypothesis in similar, but not identical, terms. Mr Crankshaw's approach is that of an English liberal; Mr Deutscher's that of a Continental neo-Marxist. But the conclusions they draw are remarkably alike, and their presenta-

tion will stand for that of other writers. I shall illustrate their
views by direct quotation from two sources: the first is a
full-page article by Mr Crankshaw in the *Observer*'s Weekend
Review for Sunday 9 September 1962; the second Mr Isaac
Deutscher's short book of lectures *The Great Contest*, published
in 1960.

In his *Observer* article, Mr Crankshaw introduces the
hypothesis in this way:

> The Soviet Union of Khrushchev is not the Soviet Union of
> Stalin, nor of Lenin. I take this as common ground. But the Soviet
> Union is still run by the Communist Party and ordered in accord-
> ance with its ideas, as it was under Stalin and Lenin. If the Soviet
> Union has changed, then the Communist Party has changed. If it
> can change a little it can change a great deal. But most people,
> including many Russians, speak and behave as though the Com-
> munist Party had not changed at all, and indeed can never
> change. It is on this assumption that our present policies are
> largely based.

But the Communist Party, argues Mr Crankshaw, *has*
changed. For example, there is Lenin's thesis that war is a
necessary prelude to world revolution:

> This thesis remained an integral part of the Communist canon
> until early in 1956, when Khrushchev, at the Twentieth Party
> Congress, formally erased it. In so doing he removed the main
> political objection to communism, as distinct from Russianism,
> and opened interesting vistas which have not yet been properly
> acknowledged by the West, much less explored.

The moral case against the Soviet system used to be strong,
writes Mr Crankshaw. But Communist methods have
changed since Stalin's death. We are faced with a very
different situation.

> The point to be made is that if Lenin's revolutionary doctrine is
> abandoned, which is certainly so, and if Stalinist militarism and
> Russian police manners are in the process of modification, which
> appears to be so, we are left with a good many things we do not
> like, some, perhaps, that are dangerous, but no longer with the

thing against which we are now armed, fixed in an attitude of implacable and eternal hostility – the Communist menace.

The 'Communist menace' has disappeared. It has been replaced by 'peaceful competition' between the two systems. Once Stalinist methods are forgotten, the new prosperous communism may win fresh sympathy among the under-developed nations:

Certainly, Mr Khrushchev is doing his best to win such sympathy. Having, as it were, outlawed war and discounted violent revolution he has put himself in a position to wait indefinitely for the Communist millenium. In Africa and in Asia he is going very quietly indeed.

Similarly, Khrushchev is encouraging a more liberal approach among the Communists in Eastern Europe:

The return to the thesis of 'different roads to socialism', propounded in 1956, but shattered by the Hungarian uprising, has been restored. Poland is pursuing a highly individual path, making accommodation with Rome, allowing all sorts of freedoms to artists and writers, turning her back on that disastrous *sine qua non* of the Communist world, the collectivization of agriculture.

The question arises, writes Mr Crankshaw, of how far communism is still communism:

It is hard to know what Mr Khrushchev believes and what he does not believe. Once upon a time he talked like a militant Leninist: this was only to be expected, considering that his way to power and his sole claim to authority rested on his capture and rejuvenation of the Communist Party apparatus, which Stalin had made sterile. Since then he has talked differently: 'We are getting richer, and when a person has more to eat he gets more democratic.'

Mr Crankshaw argues that 'communism' and 'capitalism' are in fact coming to resemble one another. If Western society has many 'socialist' elements, the East is experimenting with 'capitalist' ideas:

Soviet economists and theoreticians are casting around for ways and means of injecting some of the benefits of the Market economy into the Communist system without abandoning the central thesis that the State must own the means of production. The only sphere in which they seem irretrievably stuck is agriculture: collectivization does not work, and they know it. If that system were to be abandoned, or heavily modified, as it has been in Poland, associated changes would follow thick and fast.

What has happened in Poland is likely to be recapitulated in the Soviet Union:

It is a slow business. There are two steps backward for every three forward. Anachronisms abound. But the change is there. The Soviet Union is no longer the headquarters of a belligerent revolutionary organization stopping at nothing, including the fomenting of wars, to achieve its ends. She is no longer wedded to an immutable dogma. She has come alive.

What will the end-product be? Will it still be communism? Mr Crankshaw argues that

what the Poles have, surely, is not communism as it is understood by most of us, but the first beginnings of a new sort of system, for which we have no proper name, the future evolution of which neither we, nor the Poles, nor the Russians can foresee.

The new Russia will be an immensely powerful society; but the danger it presents will be that presented by any powerful, newly industrialized nation. While the rivalry will remain – disciplined by fear of nuclear war – our societies will come to resemble each other more and more:

It seems possible that we in the West are also, in our different ways, moving towards the same sort of system. If this is so, both East and West are making things unnecessarily difficult for themselves by insisting so loudly on the eternal opposition between communism and – what?

What indeed? For nowhere in the West today is there a true capitalist society, in the classical sense understood and defined by Marx. Nor does the West any longer represent the imperialist phase of capitalism, as defined by Lenin. We are no more a capitalist society than the Soviet Union is a Communist society.

The essence of Mr Crankshaw's thesis is that Russia, under Stalin a society utterly unlike our own, will come to resemble liberal social-democracy of the West. Mr Deutscher's argument has a different emphasis. For Mr Deutscher, capitalism remains capitalism. But the Russia of the future will be the true socialist society. Indeed, in that consists its challenge to the West. To Mr Deutscher, Stalinism was a horrific aberration from the norm of socialism. Marxism is now returning to that norm, and every increase in production will be accompanied by an increase in democratization. In the not so distant future Mr Deutscher thinks, 'the goddess of freedom' may no longer be found 'in the Western camp'. That will be the moment of greatest danger for the West. For communism will then be overwhelmingly attractive to the uncommitted world. Thus Mr Deutscher's prognosis is both more optimistic for communism, and more pessimistic for ourselves, than Mr Crankshaw's. Where Mr Crankshaw sees Russia as a liberal social-democrat, Mr Deutscher sees Russia as a libertarian neo-Marxist. His tone is correspondingly more enthusiastic (p. 39):

The last decades of Soviet history have been full of unparalleled advance and achievement and also unparalleled oppression and suffering. Hardly any other nation has ever lived through an experience so gigantic, at once so contradictory and so intense in its contradiction. This makes for an extraordinary richness of thought and feeling and for high creative tension in the nation's mind. The sense of that tension permeates the Soviet Union; watching the horizon one gets the feeling of the approach of momentous changes, of the approach of something like a historic act of birth. Russia is once again pregnant with new, world-shaking thoughts and ideas. When the present interlude is over, we shall, I am convinced, witness another flowering of the Russian intellect and culture, a flowering worthy of the traditions of Mendeleyev and Pavlov, of Tolstoy, Dostoyevsky and Chekhov, of Plekhanov, Lenin and Trotsky – a flowering which will surpass these traditions, and in which the world as well as the Soviet Union will rejoice.

What are the implications for Soviet foreign policy? At worst, the style of action has altered. Mr Deutscher writes:

Gone are the grimness, the awe-inspiring secretiveness, and the backhanded abruptness with which Soviet diplomacy acted only a few years ago.

Mr Deutscher puts down this new mildness to popular hatred of war. Indeed, the Soviet Union is compared favourably in this respect with America:

It is to the credit of Khrushchev's government that, on the whole, it has not tried to exploit the sputniks and luniks in order to foster a mood of arrogance and aggressiveness, a mood which, unfortunately, was not absent from the West during the years of the American monopoly in atomic power. Nor has Moscow so far been seized by a panicky fear that Western spies, real or imaginary, were stealing its technological secrets.

'The effect of popular pacifism on official policy,' Mr Deutscher writes, 'is powerfully reinforced by pressure for more consumer goods.' The Soviet Union has 'every reason to try and call a halt to the arms race'. 'Probably no nation lives in greater horror of nuclear war than do the Russians.' Yet the Russians, for all their new mildness, are ready to defend their social achievements. In this, Mr Khrushchev is a typical Russian of the post-Stalin era. For the Russians

still wonder to what extent capitalism remains dangerously hostile toward the Soviet Union, because it is jealous of Communist progress and fearful of its own prospects. They watch hopefully Khrushchev's diplomacy. As they see it, he has been trying hard to make good Stalin's and Molotov's mistakes. His approach and language are reasonably conciliatory; he has cut down the size of the Soviet Union's armed forces; he was the first to stop nuclear tests; he has wound up some of the Soviet military bases abroad; he took the initiative to evacuate Austria; he has exerted himself to stop the civil war in Indo-China; he has, despite opposition at home and many snubs from abroad, stubbornly persisted in his attempts to renew contacts with the leaders of the West; and he has been to the United States to proclaim the Soviet Union's desire for peace and to produce what they believe to be *the* master scheme of international disarmament. They now watch anxiously to see the result of Khrushchev's initiatives. If he achieves nothing, they will be confirmed in their worst suspicions of the West, and for all their pacific mood they would not like their government to surrender any of its vital interests.

In Mr Deutscher's view, the keynote of Khrushchev's foreign policy is 'the preservation of the *status quo*'. Such a policy implies an abstention from subversion and revolution abroad. The reason for this abstention is Russia's brilliant economic future. The Societ bloc, writes Mr Deutscher, will form

in the last quarter of this century, a single economic entity and a common 'market' four or five times larger than the North American market and at least twice as large as a common American and Western European market. Within an economic entity of that size technological progress, productivity, standardization, and mass production could develop on a scale never hitherto seen. This prospect decisively influences the general conduct of Soviet foreign affairs.

Mr Deutscher agrees with Mr Crankshaw that in Asia and Africa Khrushchev is 'going very quietly indeed':

In Iraq the Communist Party was the chief driving force of the 1958 revolution; and according to most Western observers on the spot it was quite capable of seizing power. Yet it has not even tried to do so. In taming Middle Eastern communism Khrushchev has acted in the interest of the *status quo*. His policy has undoubtedly resulted in a relative easing of the international tension in the Middle East. But no one knows how long this may last. The upheaval has hardly spent all its momentum; sooner or later it may once again take on violent forms and upset all plans based on the *status quo*. Even if the relatively calm interval is prolonged, revolutionary situations may arise elsewhere in Asia and Africa and destroy the present utterly precarious equilibrium.

But this policy of extreme restraint does not mean abandonment of Marxist aims. On this, Mr Deutscher differs radically from Mr Crankshaw:

I have said that Soviet diplomacy seeks to 'freeze' the present demarcation lines between the two blocs. For how long? Perhaps for a decade, perhaps for longer. The Soviet Union is out to gain another ten or fifteen years, in the course of which it intends to prepare for the decisive and open contest with the West. Let me explain what I mean by an 'open contest'. This need not be a test of arms. In a struggle between opposed social systems, Marxists hold, that system is bound to win which is superior in efficiency, in the ability to deploy society's productive forces and to unfold men's creative energies.

Mr Deutscher admits that this leaves the process of 'peaceful transition' from capitalism to socialism vague. The 'great contest' will apparently be a contest of example, not of arms. This vagueness consorts ill with the concreteness which – as Mr Deutscher would be the first to agree – is the essence of Leninism. Mr Deutscher does not explain how the transition is to be achieved. How is peaceful transition to be reconciled with Leninist theories of revolutionary social change? Mr Deutscher, unlike Mr Crankshaw, does *not* suggest that Khrushchev is prepared to throw Leninism overboard. Khrushchev is telling the Communists of the uncommitted world:

there is no need for you to engage immediately in any decisive struggle for power. Wait until *we* have created conditions in which you will be able to resume the struggle for power with the least danger and risk to yourselves and ourselves, conditions in which your victory will be assured.

But if the means by which increased Soviet power can contribute to the spread of communism are left vague, the prospect of increased Soviet power looms large in Mr Deutscher's account. By the end of the seventies, he believes, the Soviet Union will be 'the world's wealthiest industrial nation':

Although Soviet standards of living may still remain below the American ten years from now, they are certain to have risen above Western European standards. This will be a tremendous achievement for a people whose standards were not so long ago closer to those of China or India than of Western Europe.

The Soviet Union is already 'the world's most educated nation'. Western Europe, according to Mr Deutscher, 'is

87

working long hours'. Whereas the Russians 'are now working a 35–40 hour week' and plan to reduce this 'to 30–32 hours between 1964 and 1968'. But the West should not despair. If the challenge facing it is formidable, its resources are great:

If the West learns to face the future instead of clinging to the past, the challenge will hold no threat in it . . . competitive coexistence may yet change from the bitter competition it is to cooperative emulation.

Like Mr Crankshaw, Mr Deutscher believes that Soviet and Western societies are destined to converge. But the burden of emulation is placed firmly on the West. Though communism will grow more liberal, the West will have to emulate Communist methods to survive. Indeed, liberalization not only explains the new mildness of Russian foreign policy, it is the reason why the West has cause to fear for its future. If communism grows liberal, what will the West have to offer? Mr Deutscher concludes:

Of course, there is freedom, political freedom, in the West; and this is absent from the Soviet Union and the Communist-ruled countries. The moral importance of this contrast can hardly be over-rated. But I do not think that the contrast will last indefinitely. The Russians have already discovered that they need freedom, if only to be socially efficient. In the years to come they will discover that the doses of freedom their rulers grant them are too small and meagre. They will clamour for more and, I think, the rulers will have to meet the demand. As I see it, the coming decade will bring a gradual, or not so gradual, enlargement of civil liberty, although there will also be temporary setbacks and there may occur dramatic clashes between the rulers and the ruled.

These prospects will affect competitive coexistence. Hitherto the West has won many a moral and political battle against Russia because Russia was a tyranny and the goddess of freedom fought on the Western side. In the West were also the big industrial battalions. Now Russia is forming and marshalling her big industrial battalions; and the new Soviet generation longs to see the goddess of freedom in its camp; and it may yet tempt her over there. And then the moral advantage the West has so far enjoyed may dwindle.

CHAPTER 8

LIBERALIZATION: A CRITIQUE

THE Goddess of Freedom: is she to be tempted into the
Eastern camp? Mr Crankshaw would not go as far as that;
Mr Deutscher thinks it quite possible. The difference is
easily explained. To Mr Crankshaw, as to the rest of us, the
liberalization of Russia is a consummation devoutly to be
wished. Every retreat from Stalin is a victory for that 'liberation army of mankind' of which Heine was proud to have
been 'the good soldier'. Nobody disputes that Russia has
grown more liberal, or that this is an unmitigated good.
Mr Deutscher, however, takes the argument a stage further.
Russia today is not only more liberal than Russia in the past;
it is potentially more liberal than the capitalist West. On Mr
Deutscher's assumptions, this is not unreasonable. For Russia is not growing more liberal by a process of *embourgeoisement*, but by a process of 'revisionism'. She is returning to
that humanism which, according to Marxist 'revisionists',
is to be found at the core of Marxism. I do not think Mr
Deutscher is right. But his hypothesis is not open to the
charge that it projects Western ideas on to a foreign reality.
His hypothesis does not assume that Communists no longer
take Marxism–Leninism seriously. On the contrary, Mr
Deutscher assumes the Party will retain its ideological monopoly. But he maintains that Marxism–Leninism has the
seeds of liberalism within itself. That is how Mr Deutscher
can claim that the Goddess of Freedom may yet desert the
Western camp.

Yet the arguments employed are not dissimilar. There are
certain forces at work in Soviet society, it is said, making for

internal liberalization: particularly the rising educational and living standards. It is in our interest to encourage these forces, since internal liberalization is likely to lead to greater reasonableness in Russian behaviour abroad. Indeed, the hope of ending the Cold War depends on the triumph of these forces. As to China, it is admitted that the same forces are not – or are not yet – operative in her society. But the analogy with Stalinism suggests that China will eventually pass into a Khrushchevist phase. Meanwhile, it is in our interest to back the liberalized communism of Khrushchev against the more virulent Chinese brand. Since Russia, the more liberal power, is also indisputably the stronger, the Sino-Soviet quarrel is to be welcomed. The Soviet Union acts as a restraining influence on the more dogmatic and aggressive Chinese. These, I think, are the assumptions on which Mr Crankshaw's and Mr Deutscher's arguments rest. If they are correct, the attitudes our allies have adopted will seem wrong, or outdated. Equally, British attitudes are vindicated. How plausible, then, are these assumptions? The objections I shall raise are not based on specialist Sovietological or Sinological knowledge. In the case of Eastern Europe I can claim knowledge based on personal acquaintance. But in general my knowledge of communism is that available to the intelligent layman. This is not necessarily a disadvantage. I do not wish to challenge the factuality of Mr Deutscher's statements; though many of his claims – such as that Soviet living standards will surpass those of Western Europe by 1970 – seem to me very doubtful. A modicum of knowledge is plainly essential. But knowledge in itself is not decisive. I believe that these assumptions can be faulted on general grounds alone.

Thus, it is argued that liberalization will result from the rapid increase in Soviet educational and living standards. But what is the evidence for this? Do rising living standards and improved education *necessarily* lead to a more liberal society? What does history teach? Certainly, the history of modern Germany does not support this. Between 1870 and

1914 Germany's industrial progress was phenomenal. Her living standards rose faster than those of any European country. Her educational system was thought by many the best in the world. Like Mr Deutscher's Russians, the Germans were considered 'the world's best-educated nation'. Yet Germany between 1870 and 1914 was neither notably democratic nor notably pacific. It may be argued that Germany was a special case. Germany had a long history of autocratic government at home; Prussia was famed for belligerence abroad. But in these respects the history of Germany, different though it may be from that of France or Britain, bears a resemblance to the history of Russia. In other words, the argument from tradition is not available to the proponents of liberalization. And, significantly, they seldom appeal to it. In most Western countries, periods of autocratic government, or of extreme external belligerence, can be presented as aberrations from a norm. Western revolutionaries appeal to their contemporaries in the name of 'rights', formerly held and now in abeyance. Clearly, no Russian liberalizer is in a position to appeal to tradition in this way. (An exception might be Lenin's 'democratic centralism'. But this ideal, even if realized, would provide only for democracy within an autocratic one-party system.) Stalin is nearer the Russian norm than Kerensky. In the Russian context, hopes for liberalization are bound to be directed towards the future.

The core of the argument is in the following proposition: *that there is a necessary correlation between industrialization and democratization.* At first sight, this seems plausible enough. The great democracies of the West were the pioneers of the industrial revolution. England, at the beginning of the eighteenth century, was a pre-capitalist country ruled by an oligarchy of merchants and great landowners. Since that time, industrialization and democratization appear to have advanced hand in hand. What is true of Britain is true of America, France, Holland, Scandinavia, and the White Dominions. The inference seems plain: increased industrialization has given rise to increased democratization. It is on this analogy that Western liberals base their hopes for Russia. But is the inference sound? In the case of the democracies I have mentioned, there is little doubt that it is. The growth of a strong bourgeoisie, powerful trade unions, mass education, and mass literacy has brought greater popular participation in government. Yet there are ominous exceptions. The great industrial states are almost identical with the classical democracies – but not quite. In Germany and Japan industrialization was launched under different auspices. It was also conspicuously successful. Yet eighty years of industrialization brought Germany and Japan not to greater democracy, but to Pearl Harbour and Stalingrad. How do we explain this discrepancy?

The explanation may be quite simple. The apparent correlation between industrialization and democratization may be misleading. The true correlation may be between industrialization and *the strengthening of whatever system prevails at the onset of industrialization*. The process of industrialization does not subvert the system; it confirms it and brings out its potentialities. Thus, in a country enjoying a primitive form of democracy, industrialization will further democratic development. But in a militaristic, autocratic system, like that of nineteenth-century Germany or Japan, industrialization will strengthen anti-democratic tendencies. The prestige of industrialization accrues to the prevailing order. A look at the origins of Western democracy confirms this. In all the democracies we have mentioned free institutions *pre-date* the coming of industry. Eighteenth-century England was an oligarchy. But it was an oligarchy in which the principles of parliamentary government and individual liberty were already well grounded. In Holland, we have a parallel situation. In Switzerland, basic democratic institutions are still more ancient. America's democracy was devised long before industrialization got under way. Even in France, though it coincided with the onset of industrialization, the revolution of 1789 was not its product. It is true that Germany and Japan have developed surprisingly stable democratic systems in recent years. This suggests that democracy – contrary to what is often said – is not impossible to transplant. Indeed, the relative success of contemporary German and Japanese democracy, which has coincided with rapid industrial advance, confirms that the prestige of industrialization accrues to the order prevailing. But the argument offers little comfort to those who look to the democratization of Russia. For it was not a natural process of evolution, on which they base their hopes, that nurtured the new democracies of Japan and Germany. On the contrary, it was the violent imposition of a foreign political mould. The implications are surely profoundly disturbing.

There does not seem, then, to be any necessary correlation between democratization and industrialization. On general grounds, this is reasonable enough. The notion that political institutions are moulded by economic forces, which underlies the argument for liberalization, is Marxist in origin. It is dangerous, I think, for two reasons. First, it is deterministic: democratization is something that will come about more or less automatically, not something that individuals must fight for. It would be excellent, of course, if it were so. But nothing in English democratic experience suggests that it is so. Nor would those who put forward this argument apply it to Franco's Spain, to Verwoerd's South Africa, or to Perón's Argentina. The reason is plain. English liberals jib at applying it in these cases, because it runs counter to their sense of how democracy grew, and is maintained, in these islands. But the argument is objectionable for another reason. In its Marxist context, the notion that political institutions are the product of economic forces is bound up with a strong historical relativism. Democracy is 'historically progressive' because it marks the collapse of feudalism and the triumph of the bourgeoisie – not because it is good in itself. But a look at how European democracy came into being suggests something quite different. The democratic system seems to be compatible with a variety of economic and cultural institutions. Post-war Germany and Japan suggest that those liberals who say we cannot 'impose' institutions on those unfamiliar with them – for example, on underdeveloped nations – are too diffident. There seems to be no reason *a priori* why democracy should require any particular level of economic well-being. It is true that economic failure may, as with the Weimar republic, undermine democratic institutions. But failure discredits all political institutions, as the fate of Tsarist Russia or Wilhelmine Germany shows. Paradoxically, German and Japanese experience should be encouraging to the nations of the *tiers monde*. For it refutes any kind of determinism about the growth of democratic institutions, and suggests that their values may after all be absolute, and not relative as Marxists teach.

But if these implications are comforting for the new nations, they are less so for those who desire the democratization of Russia and China. History suggests that autocracies, while they remain successful, are self-perpetuating. Indeed, the prestige of political or economic success works in favour of the *status quo*. This is the case, after all, in democratic countries. A successful government is more likely to be returned to power than an unsuccessful one. Thus, if we rely on economic arguments alone, and argue from analogous situations in other countries, the prospects for a more liberal Russia would seem to be distinctly bad. Nor is there any *a priori* reason why the industrialized Russia of Khrushchev should be less aggressive than the backward Russia of the Tsars. The case of the industrialized autocracies of Japan and Germany suggests the opposite. But the economic argument is not usually presented in isolation. It is coupled with the argument from education. The link between the two is evident. Industrialization requires a literate, technically skilful community. A country that wishes to industrialize must therefore introduce universal, compulsory education. The experience of America, Britain, Germany, and Russia confirms that this is so. But an educated community, the

argument runs, will not tolerate methods of rule appropriate
to a backward peasant society. Education, introduced by
autocracy for purposes of industrial efficiency, will end by
undermining autocracy itself.

Stated thus baldly, the thesis is a little optimistic. But it
contains at least an important half-truth. Many of Khrushchev's liberalizing measures *can* be related to the growing
technical sophistication of Soviet society. Thus, in the Stalin
era, vast armies of slave-labour made economic sense.
Labour was cheap and plentiful. Slave-labour – with its low
productivity, but high dirigibility and indifference to wast-
age – was suitable for building railways, roads, and dams.
But Russia's reserves of peasant labour are now exhausted.
Industrial advance must be measured in terms of more complex processes: oil refining, plastics, electronics, automated
engineering. The indifference to the welfare of labour which
typified Stalin's Russia is no longer appropriate. Technical
proficiency, social insurance, financial incentives, improved
conditions of work: it is now in the regime's interest to ensure these. Whether these measures are accurately described
as liberalization is a moot point. Still, despite the poor
housing and the scarcity and inferiority of consumer goods,
these measures have made the Soviet Union a better place
to live in than it was under Stalin. A correlation between
industrialization and this kind of social advance is indis-
putable. It is also reasonable to assume that this sort of
liberalization will continue.

Nevertheless, liberalization is evidently not a happy term
for these improvements. Comparison with Bismarck's Germany, Nasser's Egypt, or Perón's Argentina shows that improved welfare can coexist with authoritarian government.
Krupps was a model of paternalistic benevolence; Bismarck
pioneered social insurance. The motivation was similar to
that in Khrushchev's Russia: technical sophistication
demanded social advance. Yet it would be inaccurate to
describe such progress as liberalization. On the contrary,
such social concessions are often made in lieu of genuine

liberalization. While industrialization can lead to better social welfare, social welfare does not necessarily lead to free institutions. Indeed, contrary to the economic determinism underlying the argument, the opposite is more nearly true. It was free institutions that enabled the working class of Western countries to fight for better conditions, and that made the oppressions of Stalinism unthinkable. We are back at our former conclusion: free institutions are not only good *per se*, but do not depend on any specific economic system. This is not to deny that some systems may be more favourable to democracy than others. But the liberalization hypothesis rests on the instrumental fallacy: that mass communications, mass literacy, technical education, higher living standards, *necessarily* produce a more liberal society. Recent controversies in this country suggest that this is fallacious. In the battle for free institutions, such factors are neutral. Television is as good a medium for propaganda as for free speech. Mass literacy can produce either a free popular press or mass indoctrination. No doubt these are truisms. It is only strange that they should be forgotten when it is Soviet society that is under discussion.

What of education in the stricter sense? Does not the very process of education encourage scepticism and free inquiry? Will the student who is taught to question other assumptions not also question the assumptions of Marxism? This argument presupposes that the intelligentsia of Eastern Europe can play in the twentieth century the role that it played in the nineteenth. The intelligentsia will be the agent of Russia's liberalization today, as it was once the agent of Russia's westernization in the nineteenth century. Although events in Hungary and Poland seem to confirm this thesis, I believe it is seriously open to question – we shall return to this point. It is tempting to object that higher education is rather more 'instrumental', and therefore more neutral, than the argument assumes. Certainly, this is true of a great deal of Soviet education. It is plain that certain types of highly original intellectual activity are easily compartmentalized. This works both ways, as is shown by Soviet and Nazi rocket expertise. These very sophisticated processes do not require a general atmosphere of freedom – they have actually flourished most brilliantly under conditions of extreme repression. What they require, evidently, is 'freedom' within their own technical parish. But this applies to a large part of the educational spectrum, particularly in a country that prides itself on its 'poly-technical' education. Here, Khrushchev's greater reluctance to impose ideological dogma on scientific activity can mislead. Certainly, it is a step in what seems to us the right direction. But it is based, like Gomulka's treatment of Polish writers, on a suspicious intellectual bargain. Intellectuals are seen to be not only most successful, *but least dangerous to Party dogma*, when given complete freedom within a compartmental framework. To the intellectual this is a welcome relief – but a doubtful compliment. For his freedom stops short at those subjects in which the Party has a direct interest: economics, sociology, historiography, philosophy. Yet these are also the 'liberal studies', the subjects in which freedom is most meaningful.

The tragedy is plain. For if Russia is to be liberalized through her intelligentsia, it is in the field of liberal studies that progress is important. What are the possibilities? Will Marxism–Leninism 'wither away', with the state it brought into being? Will Marxism–Leninism prove to be open to liberal influences from outside? Will it prove susceptible of internal regeneration? Mr Crankshaw argues that the intellectual irrelevance of Marxism, apparent to us, will soon be apparent to intelligent Marxists; indeed Mr Crankshaw maintains that this is already Khrushchev's view. Mr Deutscher's position is exactly opposed: he finds the dynamic of liberalization within Marxism itself. I believe neither view is correct, and for the same reason. Marxism is not one ideology among others: it is the doctrine on which the Communist Party is grounded and which justifies its existence. But the tendency of Khrushchev's rule has been to strengthen the Party at the expense of the other organs of state. How could the Party justify its domination of all aspects of Soviet life if it abandoned the ideology in whose name it rules?

If the growing power of the Party makes a 'withering away' of Marxism improbable, the prospects for the liberalization of Marxism itself are not good. It is no accident that 'revisionism' is the rudest word in the Party's vocabulary. What is the reason for this fear of 'revisionism'? Is it not precisely the fear that the questioning of Marxism could lead to its erosion as an intellectual system? The Party's instinct here is sound. For the teaching of the various 'revisionists' has been profoundly destructive of Marxist orthodoxy. Protagonists of liberalization (though not Mr Deutscher) are here caught in a dilemma. For, while they may regard Marxism as nonsense themselves, they cannot deny that it is the ideology on which the Party bases its legitimacy. If Marxism is true, the Party can permit questioning. But if it is false, illogical in itself, and at variance with the facts, the Party cannot afford even the most peripheral questioning. In other words, the falsity of Marxist economics, philosophy, and historiography may itself be a factor militating against liberalization.

But even if we assume that Soviet education will liberalize the new intelligentsia and not indoctrinate it, is the analogy with the nineteenth-century intelligentsia valid? There are reasons for doubting this. The intelligentsia of Eastern Europe owed its past importance to the fact that the bourgeoisie was weak or non-existent. It became the spokesman of national revival and social reform. Unlike in the West, the intelligentsia of Eastern Europe was a class in its own right, as it still is theoretically in the Soviet Union today. In fact, the intelligentsia in these countries no longer enjoys its old prestige. There has grown up a powerful, homogeneous 'new class' of bureaucrats and managers, who have given Eastern Europe the bourgeoisie she lacked in the nineteenth century. But a bourgeoisie is not necessarily a harbinger of 'bourgeois' freedoms: that is a Marxist conception. This bourgeoisie is dominated intellectually by a narrow Party dogmatism. It is given no reason to complain of economic underprivilege. The position of the intellectual in present-day Eastern Europe is more like that of the disaffected anti-bourgeois Western intellectual. Despised by the 'new class', he is no longer the authoritative spokesman of society. The Party may deal with him in more or less liberal fashion, but his social position is weak. The liberal policy Gomulka has pursued towards intellectuals is a very deliberate construction. The Party sees no danger in abstract art and electronic music. But there can be no public discussion of anything affecting basic Marxist assumptions. This is not to say that Polish intellectuals live in a fool's paradise. But they know that their freedom is as restricted as is Gomulka's own: the price of experiment at home is subservience to the Soviet Union abroad. If the intellectuals should represent a threat to the 'new class' – and what *we* call liberalization would seem a threat to this class – 'the hand of the Party', as Khrushchev told Soviet writers in 1957, 'would not tremble'.

To say that liberalization is limited is not to say it is of no value. On the contrary, the new freedom enjoyed by scientists and writers, the reduction in the power of the political police, the improvement in living standards – these gains are real and welcome. But if by liberalization we mean the creation of free institutions, the case is less clear. It is a fact that scepticism is on the increase. But will this dilute the pure milk of Party zealotry, or lead to a counter-offensive from threatened orthodoxy? The analogies drawn between Marxism–Leninism and Christianity are double-edged. How many centuries divide the forcible conversions of the fifth century from the age of Voltaire? Do not organizations depending on an all-saving ideology *alternate* between scepticism and paranoiac fanaticism? This may not prove true of Marxism; but it was certainly true of Christianity. A diastolic pattern of this kind is not certain. But it is as least as probable as a rising evolutionary curve. It corresponds to the pattern of the first forty-five years of the Soviet regime.

After the savage repressions of Civil War came Lenin's 'liberal' New Economic Policy. This was succeeded by the highly illiberal Stalinist thirties. The 'liberal' wartime years, celebrated by Pasternak, were followed by the horrors of the *Shdanovshchina* and of Stalin's final years. The Thaw of 1954–5 was succeeded by the much tougher anti-revisionist line of the later fifties . . .

I do not suggest that liberal periods are the exception, and restrictive periods the rule. It is the *precariousness* of the gains to which I want to draw attention. Indeed, that is the key. For all its autocracy, the Communist Party has made concessions to popular demand. But what autocracy gives it can also take away. The freedom Russian intellectuals now enjoy, though far more limited in degree, is not different in kind from the freedom they enjoyed under the Tsar. Without free institutions, without *habeas corpus*, an independent judiciary, and the rest, these concessions have an air of impermanence. None of these basic guarantees yet exists in Russia. The fault of the English protagonists of liberalization is that they forget, in analysing Soviet society, the lessons of our own history. Western democracy is rooted in the pluralism of Western society. But this is not paralleled in Russian society: traditional Russia recognized no dualism between Church and State. Under Stalin's rule, a degree of pluralism grew up: the economic bureaucracy, the Army, the G.P.U., the Party itself, represented distinct interests within Stalin's autocratic empire. But the chief feature of Khrushchev's rule has been the destruction of this incipient pluralism. The Party, politically inert under Stalin, is again the sole repository of power. In England, autocracy did not 'evolve' into democracy. Democracy had to be fought for. As every good democrat knows, the benefits of democracy are not even now to be taken for granted. They depend on popular vigilance, and a degree of mutual tolerance. It is not clear why in Russia, with its traditions of absolutism and arbitrary bureaucratic power, the course of democracy should be smoother.

There is a further consideration. Even if the prospects for liberalization are better than I take them to be, would a more liberal communism be less expansionist? I am not sure that abstract discussion of Communist intentions is profitable. It is better to examine the record. But the abstract argument for a more reasonable Communist foreign policy is open to the same objection as the abstract argument for liberalization. A conciliatory policy towards China is sometimes justified today on the grounds that China cannot be expansionist abroad because she is too busy at home. (The same argument was applied to the Soviet Union in the thirties.) It is likewise argued that the prosperous Soviet Union of tomorrow cannot be expansionist because she will have too much to lose. (The same argument, looking further ahead, is applied to China.) But the same considerations could be applied to any other state, at any other period in history. Does it follow that all states are either too rich or too poor to have an interest in expansion? That would require a more thorough rewriting of history than even the Communists have attempted. The truth is that the factors making for expansion cannot be reduced to an economic or ideological formula. The strong, liberal Soviet Union of the future may be theoretically less inclined to expand than the Soviet Union of Stalin. But it would be risky to argue that Soviet Russia strong is less of a threat than Soviet Russia weak. The Russia of Stalin's first years was a cruel tyranny. But it was no threat to its neighbours. Khrushchev is more liberal than Stalin. But he is also more powerful and more ambitious.

We have to consider this possibility: might not increased liberalization go with increased expansionist pressure? Does a correlation exist between internal and external relaxation? Once again, the question is not well treated in theoretical terms. But the possibility cannot be excluded. The factors making for greater confidence and freedom to manoeuvre at home *may* also be making for greater confidence and freedom to manoeuvre abroad. There is evidence, for example, that the process of *embourgeoisement* is being accompanied by a strong nationalist resurgence. Here, the story of Western imperialism provides little comfort. The period of imperialist expansion abroad coincided with increasing prosperity and democratization at home. A deliberately calculated expansionism, like that of Nazi Germany, may require regimentation and suppression of freedom. But it is never difficult for a regime that provides both material prosperity and foreign political success to win the assent of the governed. The firmer that assent, the less need a government has for organs of repression. It is arguable that just as internal criticism of imperialist policies helped to undermine the imperialist will-to-power in the West, so a more liberal Soviet Union might criticize its right to impose Communist regimes on countries beyond its borders. That is the hope. But we should not pretend that it is other than a distant and uncertain prospect.

IV. *Peaceful Coexistence or Cold War?*

CHAPTER 9

KHRUSHCHEV AND MAO

LET us build on the hypothesis that the Communists mean
what they say. They say they want to bury us: I believe
them. Khrushchev tells the Americans their grandchildren
will live under communism. I do not believe it; but I believe
Khrushchev believes it. To many, the hypothesis will seem
naïve. How can a politician believe this who is famous for his
pragmatism? It is credible of Mao Tse-tung, perhaps,
immured in his Middle Kingdom. But is it credible of
Khrushchev, who knows more about the world, and much
more about thermo-nuclear warfare? Again, has not
Khrushchev troubles enough? Encumbered with allies like
China on the one hand, and Poland, Hungary, and East
Germany on the other, can Khrushchev wish for an extension of communism? Mr Crankshaw writes:

> Mr Khrushchev . . . having, as it were, outlawed war, and dis-
> counted violent revolution . . . has put himself in a position to wait
> indefinitely for the Communist millennium. In Africa and Asia he
> is going very quietly indeed.

Mr Deutscher's view of Communist strategy differs, as we
have seen, from Mr Crankshaw's. Mr Crankshaw implied
that a strategy of world revolution had been abandoned. Mr
Deutscher took the opposite view. But his 'great contest'
was to be fought out in terms of economic and political prestige. Mr Deutscher's long-term view is therefore less optimistic for the West than Mr Crankshaw's. But his short-term
view is more optimistic. The Cold War, as we knew it in
Stalin's day, is over and done with. We can look forward to
several decades of peaceful coexistence.

Certainly, the Communists preach peaceful coexistence. But the choice between peaceful coexistence and Cold War may be a choice between words. (When, after all, did Stalin preach Cold War?) Professor Seton-Watson has written that 'Cold War and Peaceful Coexistence are not alternatives: they are two different names for the same thing.' I believe this to be true. But it does not follow that Communist strategy has not changed. Optimists and pessimists are agreed that Khrushchev does not want nuclear war. Of course, Stalin too was a cautious man: Finland and Korea were not the acts of a madman. Khrushchev is more ambitious. But he is also aware that the risks are greater; his caution is proportionate. Nevertheless, to conclude that Khrushchev has 'outlawed war, and discounted violent revolution' would be hasty. Indeed, Khrushchev himself has explicitly denied this in the case of revolutionary war. In a policy speech in January 1961 Khrushchev declared that Communists would continue to support wars of liberation in colonial countries. That this was no empty threat was clear from the renewed guerrilla fighting in South Vietnam and Laos. We shall discuss the general problem of guerrilla warfare later. Nuclear weapons have not caused Khrushchev to outlaw all types of war or even to discount violent revolution. He is anxious to avoid conventional warfare because it can so easily escalate into a nuclear exchange. But this does not apply to guerrilla tactics, which may therefore turn out to be the classical tactics of the nuclear age. But guerrilla fighting is also of its nature political. It is therefore ideally suited, as Khrushchev knows, to Communist methods and organization.

The classical Communist theory of guerrilla warfare is found in the writings of Mao Tse-tung. Lenin wrote of it; Stalin paid it little attention. It has come to seem a distinctively 'Chinese' doctrine. This has not prevented Khrushchev, as we have seen, from officially espousing it. Does this mean that Khrushchev has adopted it 'under Chinese pressure'? What kind of pressure would the Chinese be able to bring to bear upon Khrushchev? Evidently, the question is of some interest. If the nuclear stalemate can bring the 'liberal' Khrushchev to embrace so 'Chinese' a policy, perhaps *Schadenfreude* at Sino-Soviet quarrels is misplaced. Instead of Russia exerting a moderating influence on China, perhaps China may force Russia into a more combative posture. This possibility is in the logic of the situation. We have an analogy on our own doorstep. In terms of world strategy, China is to Russia as France is to the Western alliance. Like France, China is relatively weak. Though China can hope to match her partner's power in the long run (as France, without Europe, cannot), both will long remain inferior to their partners. Yet their political power is very great. Indeed, it is out of all proportion to their actual strength. Why should this be? The answer, I suggest, is that their political influence is not a function of their military or economic potential. It is a function of their indispensability to the alliance. In the case of France, it may be that she is less indispensable than she imagines. If de Gaulle should pursue what to his partners appeared a disastrous course, his bluff could be called. Nato headquarters could be transferred to Bonn or to London, and European defence based on a German–Anglo-Saxon alliance. (This is not as unrealistic as it sounds. During France's long absence in Algeria, European defence did rest precisely on a constellation of this kind.) Obviously, it would be a desperate step. But it is not inconceivable. That is why de Gaulle may be reluctant to push matters too far.

Russia is faced with a more intractable problem. For Russia is not in a position to call China's bluff. In extreme circumstances, the Western alliance might discover that France was dispensable. That choice is not open to Russia; the Soviet Union cannot afford to see China collapse. It used to be said Russia could exert influence over China by economic and other sanctions. But by withdrawing her aid and her technicians, though she has temporarily weakened China, Russia has also weakened her power of leverage. On the other hand, Chinese leverage has been in no way reduced. The complex political network of international communism remains in existence. Stalin's authority extended to the most intimate ramifications of this network. But Khrushchev has not been able to re-establish that unique authority. At home, Khrushchev may be as liberal as Mr Crankshaw and Mr Deutscher take him to be. But they do not argue that the Communist Parties outside the Soviet Union have given up all thoughts of revolution. Indeed, in claiming that Khrushchev is anxious to restrain their ardour, they assert the contrary. But a Communist Party that has ceased to pursue power by all available means – revolutionary or democratic, as the situation demands – has ceased to be a Leninist party. It has reverted to reformist social-democracy.

Is so complete an abandonment of Leninist theory at all likely? There is little evidence that it is happening, or will happen. History suggests something quite different. In any revolutionary movement – and the Communist Parties outside the Soviet Union are admitted to be revolutionary – the more militant faction is likely to have the advantage. If the Russians have really abandoned a strategy of world revolution, there can be little doubt who will win the allegiance of the world's Communist Parties. That is why any such abandonment of the goal of world revolution by the Soviet Union is improbable. The Soviet Union cannot in any circumstances allow the control of world communism to pass to China. Those who predict a more liberal future for Russia argue that Russia will restrain revolutionary ardour in China and elsewhere. Certainly, Russia has a real interest, as events in India have shown, in 'containing' Chinese expansion in Asia. But even granted the validity of the liberalization hypothesis, the logic of the argument can be reversed. It is argued that Russia will exert a restraining influence on China and world communism. I suggest that the existence of a militant Communist movement outside her borders means that Russia, even if she wished to, could not afford to pursue a policy of 'acceptance of the *status quo*'. For many years, Stalin did something very like this. He opposed a policy of 'socialism in one country' to Trotsky's 'Chinese' ambitions for world revolution. But Stalin established a personal ascendancy over the machinery of world communism. Khrushchev's control is much less complete. But 'polycentrism' does not necessarily mean greater moderation. What would Stalin have done, had he been faced not with Trotsky, but with Mao? But Khrushchev *is* faced with Mao. By competing for influence within the world Communist movement, Mao is indeed in a position to force Russia into a more combative posture.

This does not mean that Russia can be forced to accept the Chinese position lock, stock, and barrel. The Russians understand the significance of the nuclear stalemate. They will attempt – I believe with ultimate success – to instruct the Chinese in its peculiar logic. But the Chinese are correct in arguing that the nuclear stalemate need not impose a policy of 'acceptance of the *status quo*'. There are roads open to revolutionary violence below the nuclear threshhold. Guerrilla warfare is the obvious example. But there are other techniques of political infiltration and sedition in which Communist cadres are trained. Over Cuba, Kennedy's nuclear brinkmanship was successful. But the ultimate threat will not be effective if it is not credible. It requires – as in Cuba – a local superiority in conventional strength and a demonstrable determination on the part of public opinion. Nor can it be used too often. A Russian-supported Fidelist insurrection in Nicaragua might again compel America to the brink. In this theatre, therefore, Khrushchev is likely to proceed with caution. But a *coup d'état* in Ghana or Ceylon, without obvious backing from Russia, would be a different matter. Khrushchev would not expect America to react in the same way. Ghana and Ceylon are non-aligned. Neither belongs to a clearly defined Western sphere of influence. There would, naturally, be strong disincentives on Khrushchev's part to such action. Ghana and Ceylon, separated from Russian territory by thousands of miles, might be as much of an economic liability as Cuba. Again, after Cuba, the Soviets are aware of the strategic troubles far-flung acquisitions bring. But the Chinese are right to argue that the nuclear stalemate does not rule out such adventures.

It is often said that such and such 'cannot be done' because in the nuclear age it is 'simply too dangerous'. Unfortunately, nuclear stalemate between Russia and America does not seem to have brought that kind of stability. I sympathize with those who see in a Soviet–American condominium the best hope for world peace. But I believe they are wrong to base their hopes on the Soviet doctrine of peaceful coexistence. For, as defined by the Russians – and *a fortiori* by the Chinese – it excludes 'ideological coexistence', but not revolutionary warfare. Yet a meaningful condominium would have to imply a genuine 'acceptance of the *status quo*'. Not only would the two powers have to agree not to go to war against one another, and to stamp out conflicts between minor powers, but the principle of non-interference in each other's spheres of influence would have to be rigorously applied. By this logic, the West would have to abandon its efforts to subvert the Communist world (as it has long since done in practice), or even to influence it by propaganda. Equally, the Communists would have to abandon the apparatus of subversion they maintain in the West. Nothing short of this could ensure lasting stability and rule out mistrust between the two super-powers. But this is a utopian prospect. It is a demand that the world's Communist Parties should go out of business. The unlikelihood of any lasting Communist 'acceptance of the *status quo*' is apparent. (There might also be resistance in some circles in the West: but in practice the West has long 'accepted the *status quo*' as far as the Communist world is concerned.) I conclude that as long as peaceful coexistence means to the Communists what it does, the political basis for a condominium is lacking. This is not due to any particular 'misunderstanding' or 'mistrust' between the great powers, such as a summit conference could disperse, but to the nature of communism. To expect a Communist to 'accept the *status quo*' is to ask him to change his nature.

In the following chapters I shall examine certain situations that have arisen in the course of the Cold War and are likely to arise again. They are chosen not because they are important in themselves (though many *are* important in themselves), but because they are typical. Berlin; Cuba; India; Vietnam; Malaya: each is a different challenge requiring a separate response. Not all concern Britain directly; but all concern Britain by implication. Our malaise is not the product of the Cold War. It has its roots in our 'lost imperial heritage', in our 'antiquated social structure'. But I believe our misunderstanding of the Cold War is a product of that malaise. We do not see the world with the same eyes as our allies in America and Europe. This book is a critique of the British view of the Cold War. But a just appreciation of the Cold War does not amount to a 'national purpose'. It is only the Communist nations, and a minority in them, who can find a national purpose in the Cold War. For the West, the Cold War is a defensive struggle. Indeed, that is the root of the trouble. A defensive posture is likely to demoralize. In Berlin and elsewhere, many Westerners – but especially ourselves – have found demoralizing this passivity in the face of provocation, this inability ever to hit back. We have no alternative but to adopt this stance. Nevertheless, if an understanding of the Cold War cannot provide us with a 'national purpose' (or at most with a negative one), it can provide us with an understanding of the context in which decisions must be made. Where the Common Market and the Atlantic alliance are concerned, a correct appreciation of the Cold War is essential. Would 'going into Europe' have meant joining a 'Cold War grouping'? Or would a stronger Europe be a deterrent to Soviet expansionism? These problems exist in the context of the Cold War. Nor is our policy towards the underdeveloped countries unaffected by our attitude; without the Cold War the concept of non-alignment would not have come into existence. I believe that our allies have understood that context better than we have. Paradoxically, however, their less optimistic view of communism has not led them to a pessimistic view of their own prospects. It is we, committed to optimism, who have suffered the decline in confidence, the doubts and hesitations about our future. The reversal is not without irony.

CHAPTER 10

'LES INCERTITUDES ANGLAISES'

BRITAIN in the Cold War: what has our role been? Are we America's Candid Friend? Her Staunchest Ally? Are we 'soft on communism'? Are we the 'Greeks of the American Empire'? Are we the Honest Broker between East and West? Are we *perfide Albion*? Evidently, we have a mixed reputation. We have been all things to all men, a universal scapegoat. But we have learnt that we cannot be all things to all men simultaneously. Honest Broker cannot also be Staunchest Ally. What is candour for the goose may be perfidy for the gander. Greeks are feared, especially when bearing gifts. Rome adores Greek culture; but Greek advice on strategy is no longer in demand. 'Britain has lost an Empire and not yet found a role,' said Mr Acheson unkindly. Was it a fair judgement? Moscow; Nassau; Brussels: our hesitations suggest that it was. *Les incertitudes allemandes*, the French used to say. But what of *les incertitudes anglaises*? Of course, Albion is not really *perfide*, only muddled; the French are too rational to understand that. We would be America's Candid Friend; but we resent American candour towards Britain. Towards Moscow the Germans should be flexible; towards Paris they should be intransigent. Europe; America; the Commonwealth: where does John Bull belong?

This confusion is something new. It was not there twenty, fifteen, even ten years ago. Twenty years ago, we knew that Hitler had to be defeated; there was no confusion about that. Fifteen years ago, we knew that Stalin meant to take Berlin; there was no hesitation then. When the Communists attacked in Korea, Britain fought at America's side. There was criticism of American tactics; but Britain's strategic role was not in question. The British Army was still the second strongest in the West; our strength was limited, but indispensable. While Ernest Bevin was her Foreign Secretary, Britain was not accused of being soft on communism: she was more often accused of being too hard. That is why the record for the immediate post-war period is worth re-examining. For far from being soft on communism it shows Britain in America's shoes. It was Churchill who warned against Soviet designs in Eastern Europe; Roosevelt and his advisers who trusted Stalin. In December 1944, Britain intervened in Greece to prevent a Communist take-over – against American advice. Americans feared that a socialist Britain might be sympathetic to Russia. Yet as early as 20 August 1945 Bevin was criticizing the unrepresentative nature of the new governments of Romania, Bulgaria, and Hungary in the House of Commons. There was no rift as yet in the Soviet–American honeymoon. In his *British Foreign Policy since the Second World War*, Mr C. M. Woodhouse remarks of that period:

Up to that point the brunt of the growing tensions between the Western powers and the Soviet government had been borne by the British. The United States was not under attack at all in the U.N. in the early days, nor did American representatives take the lead in criticizing others. When, for instance, the Soviet government pressed its claim for a revision of the Montreux Convention of 1936 on the Turkish Straits, it was Bevin who resisted them ... At the Foreign Minister's Conferences in the summer of 1946, Bevin again took the lead on the Western side, *as was natural since the matters under discussion were specifically European*: for instance, the Danube Commission, the friction between Italy and Yugoslavia, the Austria Peace treaty ... [My italics.]

It is easily forgotten how great Britain's responsibilities still were, and how small her transatlantic ally's desire to share them:

Among the non-Communist countries, Britain's special position was particularly recognized in south-east Europe. A new Turkish

Prime Minister referred in August 1946 to the Anglo–Turkish Alliance as the principal basis of Turkey's foreign policy. Greece was economically, militarily, and politically almost a dependency of Britain. Both these countries were to become within two years part of the United States' sphere of interest. But no such sphere existed in Europe in 1946. Up to the end of that year, the main American object in Europe was to withdraw from it as soon as possible.

Nor was Britain's role as the shock-absorber of Communist pressure confined to Europe. After the Japanese surrender, Britain was confronted with a Greek situation in the East: Communist and nationalist guerrillas had seized power in Burma, Malaya, Vietnam, and Indonesia. The latter responsibilities were handed back – for better or for worse – to the French and the Dutch. But in Malaya Britain had a twelve-year Emergency on her hands. Similarly, in China it was Britain that bore the brunt of the Communist advance. British business was severely hit. A British ship, H.M.S. *Amethyst*, was attacked by the Communists on the Yangtse. Indeed, American Asian policy up to the outbreak of the Korean war in June 1950 was remarkably like American European policy up to 1947:

There was little enthusiasm in their response to Chiang Kaishek's request for more military aid in November 1948. . . . The general policy was to wait and see. . . . U.S. policy remained noncommittal for the rest of 1949. . . . In response to rumours, the Secretary of State denied any intention of taking part in any Pacific defence pact in May. In August the U.S. government published a White Paper on the Chinese situation, putting the blame on the Kuomintang. Others, nearer to the scene of action, reacted less academically. President Quirini of the Philippines addressed a warning to the U.S. Senate of the threat to Asia a few days later. But even in December 1949, the month in which Mao Tse-tung first visited Moscow as head of the Chinese people's government, the State Department circulated a confidential memorandum discounting the importance of Formosa. . . .

In January 1950, Britain recognized the Communist

government of China – a course dictated largely by business interests. This act of recognition, though it did Britain little good, became the single most bitter source of discord between America and Britain during the fifties. In view of this, Mr Woodhouse's appraisal of American policy at the time is of some interest:

In January 1950 ... Acheson made a statement to the Senate Foreign Relations Committee which clearly implied that both Formosa and Korea were outside the United States' essential defence perimeter. There was still even a possibility that the U.S. might recognize the new Chinese government. Some American business interests urged the Government to do so ... these hopes proved illusory, but at least were not yet regarded in the U.S.A. as treasonable. .... *The Americans had not yet begun to think of strategy in global terms.* [My italics.]

Britain had not the strength to influence the course of events in the Far East. But the difference between American and British policy in the area was not that America was 'hard' and Britain 'soft'. At that time, the difference was marginal. But the area lay, after all, within an American sphere of influence. It was America's hesitations and confusions, not Britain's, that encouraged Communist aggression in Korea.

I have said that the Second World War caused Britain and America to exchange roles. As the old American isolationism had depended on the Royal Navy, so the new British isolationism depended on America's nuclear and conventional power. I believe this to be true of the past ten or fifteen years. But it was evidently not true of the immediate post-war period. It was the British, under Churchill and Bevin, who were the first to resist Communist pressure. It was the Americans who, to the applause of the old isolationists under Taft, wished to withdraw from foreign commitments. Rooseveltian illusions about Russia combined with Republican isolationism to weaken America's stand. America possessed one card which the Russians knew to be a trump: the atomic bomb. It is not pleasant to speculate what might have happened in Europe during the phase of maximum Soviet aggressiveness (1947–50) had the West lacked that deterrent. Europe itself could offer no serious resistance. A West German contribution to Europe's defence was still ten years away. There was no Italian army. Spain was outlawed. The forces of Belgium, France, and Holland were being painfully rebuilt. The only obstacle between the Red Army and the Channel ports was the depleted strength of the Anglo-Saxon powers. Of these powers it was Britain that was most closely affected. The role of protector of Europe fell naturally to her. Since Stalin looked forward to a complete American withdrawal, it was for the British that his thunderbolts were reserved. It was in Stalin's interest to conciliate the Americans. To us, the situation is not without irony. What General de Gaulle aspires to become before the end of this decade, Britain actually was in the first post-war years; the protector of Europe's interests. The logic is similar: since America's future involvement in Europe is uncertain, a European power must assume the role of protector. But this protector must have control over the ultimate weapons. That was the Attlee government's argument in 1946: it is de Gaulle's argument today.

In Asia it was five years before American involvement was complete. In Europe the period was shorter. The point at which Britain abdicated her protecting role, and America assumed it, can be exactly dated. The winter of 1946–7 was a bad one for Britain. The full extent of Britain's post-war economic weakness was revealed. Circumstances demanded that Britain play a great-power role in Europe, the eastern Mediterranean, India, and south-east Asia. But Britain no longer had the strength to play such a role. A programme of devolution became necessary. In February 1947 the British government informed the American government that it could no longer afford its commitments in Greece. This was forcing America's hand with a vengeance. Without Western help, the Communist guerrillas might win control of the country. The American response was swift. On 12 March the Truman Doctrine committed America to the containment of communism in Greece and Turkey. A reversal of America's post-war policy of disengagement began. For both Anglo-Saxon powers, then, 1947 was the pivotal year. Britain disengaged herself from imperial commitments in India, Pakistan, Burma, and Ceylon. In the Middle East, Britain's disengagement from Iraq and Palestine was foreshadowed. Her withdrawal into the Suez Canal Zone began. Where Britain disengaged, America moved in. On 5 June the Secretary of State, General Marshall, outlined an American recovery plan for Europe. Ernest Bevin responded to the American initiative. Europe's economic recovery, which was to check the internal Communist threat, could now get under way. In July George Kennan, in an article in *Foreign Affairs*, defined a new American doctrine: 'containment'. The burden of resistance to Communist pressure had passed out of British hands.

Having taken up the challenge, America pursued it with a vigour that alarmed her ally. The roles were now reversed. Before, America had urged restraint and conciliation towards Russia. She had criticized Britain's 'provocative activities' in Greece, Turkey, and south-east Asia. Now the boot was on the other foot. In future Britain would urge restraint and conciliation at every turn, to the chagrin and frustration of her ally. Indeed, so completely has that first post-war phase been forgotten that this now seems the 'natural' relationship between America and Britain. The Special Relationship invokes an image of Britain as Candid Friend and Wise Counsellor. America may be respected for her vigour. But her callowness and hysteria are contrasted with British political wisdom. Let us look at the cases that are cited to illustrate the workings of the Special Relationship: Britain, it is said,

> intervened to prevent General MacArthur using nuclear weapons against China during the Korean War (Attlee's flight to Washington in December 1950);

restrained America from using nuclear weapons, or otherwise intervening, at the time of Dien Bien Phu (Eden and Dulles's London meeting in April 1954);

took the initiative in exploring Khrushchev's intentions, and in coaxing the Americans towards a summit, after Khrushchev's Berlin speech of November 1958 (Macmillan's visit to Moscow in January 1959).

Now these initiatives may or may not have been well-advised. But they represent a pattern. The chief responsibility for resisting Communist pressure falls to America. In general, Britain stands with America against communism. But Britain is also a free agent. She will therefore differ at times from America. These examples show that she has done so. But the examples have one feature in common: they are all *negative*. Britain is presented always as *restraining America from doing something*. Britain is presented always as persuading America to make concessions, never as persuading her to take a firmer stand. In no case is Britain credited with urging America to confront Communist power more resolutely. (An exception might be Suez; but of the few who would still defend Suez, even fewer would defend it on these grounds.)

If this has come to seem the 'natural' role for Britain, the reason is not far to seek. The minor partner in an alliance cannot initiate a forward policy without the backing of the major partner. Yet once that policy is decided, the role of the minor partner will be auxiliary. Thus it was on a British motion in the Security Council that the United Nations intervened in Korea. But once intervention had begun, Britain found herself less and less consulted on the conduct of the war. The minor partner in an alliance has a dispiriting role. On the other hand, the minor partner has a power of veto. Even if its assistance is not strictly essential – as in Korea – the major partner will think twice before it splits the alliance. If the minor partner is strategically situated, or politically indispensable, it can exert considerable leverage. We have examined the logic of this in the case of

France and of China. Here the logic is reversed. The minor partner is the less militant partner. But this is often likely to be so. The minor partner has more reason to fear a forward policy than the major. This was certainly true of Britain. To the minor partner a 'negative' role is likely to be attractive: it ministers simultaneously to its fear of involvement and to its self-esteem. I am not saying that a 'negative' role is not at times useful and important. But a nation regarding this as its 'natural' role will develop a defensive, defeatist mentality. I believe that this is what has happened in Britain since 1947. But Americans who see in this mentality a symptom of British decadence are wrong. This mentality is the product of Britain's situation in the world.

I shall discuss Britain's role in the post-1958 Berlin crisis in a moment. By then this image was firmly established in the public mind. But what of the other examples? What truth is there in the legend of a 'hot-headed America' being brought to reason, at the time of Attlee's visit to President Truman? No case is more frequently instanced to justify Britain's role. Yet what happened? Let me quote from a review of the Truman memoirs by Mr R. H. S. Crossman (*The Charm of Politics*, p. 24):

Mr Attlee, it will be remembered, suddenly decided to go to Washington owing to a rumour that General MacArthur was to be permitted to use atomic weapons in Korea. According to Mr Truman, they got on fine, agreeing at once that there could neither be a voluntary evacuation of Korea nor a spreading of the war. Characteristically, Mr Attlee seems to have been content to assure himself that the President was in control. Apparently he never mentioned General MacArthur and his only reference to the atomic bomb was made in an aside when the conference was over and the communiqué actually being drafted .... If this picture is correct, British Socialists should undertake some rethinking. We have all made speeches about the Labour government's moral influence in Washington and the restraint it exercised on America's wild men. In fact, these claims fail to do credit to the courage and will-power of Harry Truman. The President, on his own initiative, exercised both the moral influence and the restraint.

Mr Crossman's conclusion is surely just. Not only is the story of British intervention exaggerated, its implications are as insulting to our ally as they are flattering to ourselves.

The change that Britain's image of her role in the Cold War underwent between 1948 and 1958 is most striking in regard to Berlin. Over China, Britain's differences with her ally continued in principle. In practice, Britain did not openly challenge American policy. This was a matter on which Americans were liable to anti-British sentiment. Over Germany, on the other hand, British and American opinion were to grow far apart. During the first Berlin blockade (June 1948–May 1949) Britain had given America full backing. Public opinion understood the challenge. There was general support for the air lift, in which many R.A.F. crews lost their lives. The blockade proved unsuccessful, and was called off a year later. The Russians saw that strong-arm methods in Czechoslovakia and Germany were losing them popular support. In fact, the Russians had provoked the thing they most wished to prevent: an American commitment to Europe. The collapse of the blockade ended the first post-war Communist offensive in Europe. The Iron Curtain was clamped down, except in Austria and in Berlin itself. The Greek adventure was abandoned.

The active phase of this offensive had lasted scarcely two years. It had been wholly disastrous for the Communists. Eastern Europe had been consolidated – but at the price of losing the political initiative in Western Europe, and in Western Germany. The Communists had shown their hand too early. The insurrectionary strikes in France and the flood of revolutionary violence in Italy alienated potential supporters of a Popular Front. West Germany was now bitterly anti-Communist. The Western powers were committed to the formation of a viable West German state. With this stalemate in Europe, the first phase of the offensive ended. The second phase was in a theatre where American power was not yet fully committed: south-east Asia and the Far East. Though the Russians had given little direct encouragement to the Chinese Communist revolution, there is small doubt that their plans were coordinated with Mao. The wave of political violence that swept Indonesia, India, Burma, Malaya, culminating in the Korean aggression, was the continuation of the abortive offensive in Europe. As in Berlin, it was stopped by the prompt and forceful – and clearly unexpected – American response in Korea, which had the backing of the British government and of the majority of British opinion. With the Korean armistice of 1953, and the Geneva agreements on Indo-China in 1954, the first and most violent phase of the Cold War came to an end.

Yet the first cracks in Anglo-American solidarity had made their appearance by 1950. There was the disquiet over General MacArthur's policies in Korea. But the Far East was no longer a prime concern of British policy or public opinion. It was the German question that brought the conflict into the open. America was convinced that the Russian threat could only be met by re-arming Germany. In the aftermath of Korea this became official American policy. What was Britain to do? The repugnance to British sentiment of re-arming Germany was evident. To the Americans, a revived, re-armed Germany would be a useful minor partner. To the British, a revived, re-armed Germany would be a major rival. Though memories of Nazism played their part, I believe that this consideration underlay British repugnance. But it is important to distinguish government policy from public sentiment. Officially, Britain followed the American line. Indeed, Churchill first suggested a German contribution to the European army. When the European Defence Community collapsed in August 1954, Eden negotiated West Germany's admission to Nato. Officially, the British government is as committed today to the reunification of Germany and the recognition of Bonn as the sole successor to the Reich (which implies non-recognition of other claimants) as it was in 1949. But the gap between official policy and public sentiment has steadily grown. In 1949, at the time of the Berlin blockade, there was remarkably little anti-German sentiment in Britain. Nazi Germany had been defeated. The British were prepared to believe that Germany had turned over a new leaf. The response to public appeals to feed German children and assist German refugees suggested that the British – none too well-off themselves – were willing to be generous in victory. There was admiration for the Berliners' courage and endurance. When the Bonn republic was founded in 1949, even traditional anti-Germans like Lord Vansittart gave it their blessing.

Yet, from 1950 onward, anti-German sentiment began to grow. Foreign observers have pointed to this new anti-Germanism as a key feature of Britain in the fifties. Indeed, it became so all-pervading as to be taken for granted. Like Britain's position as the recalcitrant minor partner in the Anglo-American alliance, it came to be considered 'natural'. At first sight, this might appear a common-sense reaction. After all, Britain had suffered terribly in the war. She had reason to be beastly to the Germans. But comparison with other countries casts doubt on the 'naturalness' of this British reaction. In America, the Bonn republic was accepted from the first by public opinion as an important experiment in German democracy. By 1953, when it was evident that the experiment had succeeded, American feeling towards anti-Communist West Germany verged on the enthusiastic. The war had been forgotten. West Germany was accepted as the equal of America's other European allies, Britain and France. Though the earlier enthusiasm has cooled, this remains the basic American view.

America's reactions, it may be said, are untypical. America did not suffer Nazi bombing or threats of invasion. But comparison with Europe only emphasizes British isolation. If Britain had suffered, others had suffered more. Yet anti-German feeling was stronger in Britain than in many of the countries occupied by Hitler. One explanation given for this anti-German feeling was fear of neo-Nazism. In fact, as all observers agree, the threat to German democracy from the extreme Right, which many expected, failed to materialize. The hold of the major democratic parties on the nation's political life has grown stronger. The disastrous pattern of the Weimar Republic had been reversed. Most of Germany's neighbours – though not her neighbours to the East – have been quick to recognize this. If they are anti-German, it is for reasons that have little to do with fear of neo-Nazism. Indeed, it is not clear that a correlation exists between current anti-Germanism and the degree of a nation's suffering under the Nazis. Denmark and Norway suffered, relatively speaking, rather little. Yet both are extremely anti-German. France suffered far more. Yet French fears of Germany declined during the fifties. Britain did not suffer as much as any of the countries physically occupied by the Germans. And Britain was, by European standards, pro-German after 1945. Yet Britain has fostered since 1950 – particularly on the far Right and on the far Left – the most vicious anti-Germanism outside the Communist bloc.

What is the explanation? It is, I think, that anti-Germanism has rather more to do with *les incertitudes anglaises* than with alleged fears of neo-Nazism. This is confirmed by a curious fact. British anti-Germanism in the fifties went unreciprocated. After 1958, there was bitterness in Germany about British conciliatoriness towards Khrushchev. Dr Adenauer, never a friend of Britain, did not hide his hostility. But the general tone of German comment on Britain was friendly enough. Britain was widely admired and respected at all levels of society. The German response to the collapse of the Common Market negotiations has shown how isolated Dr Adenauer was in his hostility to Britain. Britain's anti-Germanism in the fifties is to be understood, I believe, in terms of Britain's own malaise. Ironically, it is General de Gaulle who has given this particular phobia its death-blow. He has provided Britain with a real opponent in place of a dummy.

CHAPTER II

BERLIN AND ALL THAT

BRITISH anti-Germanism in the fifties was a baffling
phenomenon. But it would have had no political significance
had Khrushchev not renewed the Berlin challenge in
November 1958. I shall not describe the course of this
second Berlin crisis in detail. Its general features are familiar
enough; for the details I may be allowed to refer the reader
to my *Berlin: Hostage for the West*. For our purposes, it is the
strategy underlying the new Communist offensive that is
important. Was the new Communist strategy offensive – as
the pessimists claim? Or was it basically defensive – as the
optimists claim? On this, opinions are divided. In this
country, on the whole, the optimists have been in the
majority. *Berlin: Hostage for the West* was a statement of the
pessimistic view. I believe that the year 1958 saw a world-
wide renewal of Communist activity. Between 1952 and
1958, a time of uncertainty and vacillation in the Kremlin,
Communist activity was relatively quiescent. The only important exception was the sending of arms to Egypt in the
autumn of 1955. This brought Soviet power to bear in a
theatre where Stalin would not have dreamed of interfer-
ing. It was a pointer to the wider ambitions of Khrushchev's
Russia. Certainly, it was not consistent with a desire 'to
preserve the *status quo*' in the Middle East. In the event, the
results were more dramatic than the Russians could reasonably have expected: the world had the Suez crisis on its
hands. Still, the convulsions in the Middle East, from Suez
to the 1958 revolution in Iraq, brought the Russians little
direct profit. Indeed, a Communist take-over is today less
likely in any of these countries than it was ten years ago.

This piece of calculated trouble-making was not typical of the period 1952–8. The failure of the 1947–52 offensive in Berlin, and then in Korea, showed the dangers of a strategy of direct approach. The Kremlin had to rethink its policy. The result was the promulgation of the doctrine of 'peaceful coexistence'. This doctrine is often thought to be a product of the liberalizing post-Stalin phase. But this does not fit the chronology. The new strategy had been hammered out before Stalin's death, and by Stalin himself. It is plain in Stalin's essay *Economic Problems of Socialism in the U.S.S.R.*, which was written early in 1952 and presented to the 19th Congress of the Communist Party in October. Against Lenin's theoretical view that

the contradictions between capitalism and socialism are stronger than the contradictions among the capitalist countries

(which implies that the Western countries are more likely to attack the Soviet Union than to attack one another), Stalin argued that war

with the U.S.S.R. . . . is more dangerous to capitalism than war between the capitalist countries: for whereas war between capitalist countries puts in question only the supremacy of certain capitalist countries over others, war with the U.S.S.R. must put in question the existence of capitalism itself.

And this is the theoretical basis of the doctrine of peaceful coexistence. Thus it was really Stalin who, in Mr Crankshaw's phrase, 'abolished war' – not Khrushchev. Berlin and Korea had shown the Communists two things: outright war against the capitalist powers was too dangerous; on the other hand, the Sino-Soviet bloc was now for all practical purposes invincible. As Soviet nuclear power grew – the first Soviet test had been in August 1949 – the fear of an attack from the West, with which the early Bolsheviks had been obsessed, finally receded. In this new situation of stalemate, the Communist strategy had to be one of indirect approach. By supporting anti-colonialism, the new states must be won for the Communist cause. The sending of arms to Egypt was the most aggressive expression of this new policy. More typical was the visit of Khrushchev and Bulganin to India and south-east Asia in 1955 (though it was the Chinese who pursued this policy with greater subtlety: Chou En-lai's personal success at the Bandung Conference seems to have impressed Asians more than the Soviet Union's ham-fisted, and rather belated, anti-colonialism).

That it was Stalin who initiated this new policy provokes two reflections. In origin, *peaceful coexistence was not in any way related to liberalization within the Soviet Union*. On the contrary, 1952 was a year of savage repression in the Soviet Union and Eastern Europe. The 'Jewish Doctors' plot', and many other signs, suggested that a new blood purge was in the making. Yet it was this same half-mad, blood-crazed Stalin who laid the foundations of the doctrine of peaceful coexistence. This provokes a further reflection. If liberalization did not bring about the switch in Communist tactics, what did? The answer lies, I suggest, in the relative failure of the 1947–52 offensives in Asia and Europe. But if these offensives failed, it was not for lack of effort. They failed because they came up against the superior power of the West. It is often asked in what way the West can hope to influence Communist policy. Here, ironically, the West had found a way. *A more moderate policy had been forced on the Communists by a vigorous Western response*. It was not the result of greater liberalization within the Soviet Union. In dealing with the Communists, strength had proved remarkably educative. The implications for 'civilizing' Russian and Chinese ambitions in the future should be evident.

Peaceful coexistence was appropriate during the period 1952–8 for other reasons. America's nuclear preponderance was still considerable. The succession crisis within the Kremlin had not been settled. Both of these factors were eliminated during the autmn of 1957. Khrushchev removed his last important rival, Zhukov, from the Party Presidium. The success of the sputnik showed that Russia would soon be in a position to threaten America. Centrifugal tendencies in Russia and in Eastern Europe had been checked. 'Revisionism' was in retreat. In Poland, Gomulka had won a measure of internal autonomy, though at the price of subservience to Moscow abroad. With the affairs of the Communist bloc in reasonable order, and America in the grip of a serious recession, the stage seemed set for another period of advance. There was the Turkish crisis in the autumn of 1957; the Middle Eastern crisis in July 1958. The Quemoy crisis of August 1958 led on to the second Berlin crisis in November. Between 1958 and 1961 the guerrilla campaigns in Laos and South Vietnam were renewed; the infiltration and satellization of Cuba completed. In June 1961, at Vienna, Khrushchev presented Kennedy with a fresh Berlin ultimatum. In August came the Berlin Wall and the virtual annexation of East Berlin.

Looking back, the period 1957–62 bears all the marks of a coordinated campaign, comparable to the offensive of 1947–52. At the time of writing (May 1963), the most acute phase of the offensive appears to be over. The Cuba débâcle of October 1962 seems to have forced a pause, possibly a temporary armistice. That may prove too optimistic an assessment. But the indications, in the late summer of 1962, were that Khrushchev intended to bring the Berlin crisis to a head after the Congressional elections in November. The purpose of the erection of missile sites in Cuba during September and October was to have a bargaining counter in hand when the crisis broke. In a sense, then, Khrushchev only built his missile sites in order to remove them – though he intended to remove them at his leisure, after he had won a political victory. In the event, the trap was sprung. Khrushchev had lost the initiative. No peace treaty was signed with East Germany. The test of strength planned for November 1962 was called off. In January 1963, at the East German Party conference, Khrushchev declared that the Wall had made a solution less urgent. For the time being, the Berlin crisis had ended with a whimper.

The later offensive resembled the earlier in certain important respects. At the outset, the situations of Stalin and Khrushchev were not dissimilar. Both stood at the end of a phase of concentration and coordination within the Communist bloc. In Stalin's case, the satellization of Eastern Europe had been completed, the ideological relaxation of wartime Russia reversed, by the summer of 1947. Ten years later, Khrushchev's dominions had undergone a similar process. In terms of personal ambition, Stalin and Khrushchev were impatient men. Both were in their late sixties. Both were conscious of the immense power in their hands and of the need to use it while the balance was still favourable. Yet both offensives were comparative failures. The results of the first were meagre: Stalin won Czechoslovakia, but not Germany or Korea (North Vietnam and China were Ho's and Mao's victories, not Stalin's). The victories in the second offensive were no less meagre, and only indirectly of Khrushchev's making: Cuba and Laos. Both offensives, of course, were bedevilled by troubles within the camp. Stalin's plans were complicated by Tito's disaffection; Khrushchev's by the rift with China.

Why did these offensives fail? The question is of some interest, since on a correct answer to it depend our chances of preventing a repetition and of meeting it should it come. The answer is not really in doubt. Both offensives failed for the same reason: the Communists overestimated their own resources and underestimated those of the enemy. In his calculations, Stalin did not allow for the Marshall Plan, for the air lift, for American intervention in Korea. Psychologically, Khrushchev did not allow for the resolution of the Kennedy administration (it is plain that he took the Bay of Pigs episode for a sign of weakness). Materially, Khrushchev did not allow for America's ability to catch up in the arms race, particularly in the field of ballistic missiles. He did not see that America was in a position to dictate, without harm to herself, a pace that might be ruinous to the Soviet Union. Soviet strategy, under both Stalin and Khrushchev, had been the same: to make gains at the expense of the West without provoking a response disproportionate to the gains. Yet both offensives did just that. By overreaching themselves, instead of accelerating the centrifugal forces in the enemy camp, they brought new centripetal forces into being. At the same time, the centrifugal forces in their own camp grew more menacing. At this point, where it starts to bring diminishing returns, the prudent general breaks off an offensive. That is what Stalin did in 1952. It is what Khrushchev appears to have done ten years later.

How does this relate to our double theme: to Berlin, and to Britain's posture in the Cold War? There can be no doubt that Berlin and the German question were the main objectives of Khrushchev's offensive. If he has temporarily failed, it is important to know what led to this failure and what role Britain played in the process. The third Berlin crisis that began in Vienna in June 1961 provides a test of Britain's posture in the Cold War, and of its efficacy. The facts are available and not in doubt. Britain's posture differed from that of her main allies. The British government, and even more British opinion, inclined from the first to conciliation and negotiation. The American government, on the other hand, and to a lesser extent the French and German governments, was under powerful pressure from public opinion to 'stand up to the Russians'. Which attitude was correct? In these matters it is important not to be dogmatic: each attitude may be appropriate at a different time. To some extent it is a question of tactics. On the whole, by steering a middle course between 'strength' and 'conciliation' during 1961, I believe President Kennedy acted wisely – though it should be noted that it took the Cuba showdown a year later to bring the crisis to an end.

But what of Britain's role? It is often argued that by her 'flexibility' Britain kept the door open for negotiations. But this argument is not satisfactory. In what sense, after all, was the door ever closed to negotiations? It is a naïve view that it requires a summit conference for heads of state to communicate with one another. The normal channels of diplo-

matic communication are always open. In the context of the
alliance Britain's flexibility perhaps had its value. It may be
argued that Britain's flexibility balanced French and German rigidity. But if this generous and panoptic view is open
to the outsider, it is not open to ourselves. Policies recommended by British commentators were not recommended
for Britain alone. They were recommended for the Western
alliance. What would have happened if Western policy had
been in Britain's hands rather than in those of the United
States? Would Khrushchev have called off his offensive? Or
would the prospect of negotiations have whetted his appetite? After June 1961, America too offered negotiations. But
she also recalled 125,000 men to the colours, airlifted a division to Europe, spent large sums on civil defence, asked two
and a half million dollars more for her armed forces. Britain
merely offered negotiations. She made no move at all to
improve her military strength. That was the difference between the British and American reactions. In both countries,
it should be noted, governments had public opinion on
their side. President Kennedy expressed American willingness to defend Berlin, if necessary by force. From the Glen-
eagles Golf Club, Mr Macmillan was heard to declare that
the crisis had 'all been got up by the Press'.

It was said, during Cuba Week, that the crisis was no
direct concern of Britain's: Cuba was an American problem.
But this could not be said of Berlin and Germany. In Berlin,
Britain was one of the occupying powers, whose responsibility for reunifying Germany was a major element in the
crisis. Britain had a large army in Germany. Any change in
the political or military situation in Central Europe must
affect her own security. It was clear from the start that Berlin
was not Khrushchev's only aim. Indeed, it appeared that it
might not be his primary aim. He would have liked to expel
the West from Berlin. But he knew that this would be too
dangerous. In addition, while Western troops remained, he
had a lever by which other concessions might be extracted:
acceptance of the Oder–Neisse frontier, a ban on nuclear

weapons for the Bundeswehr, recognition of the East German republic. I argued in *Berlin: Hostage for the West* that there was a distinct priority in these demands. Khrushchev cannot be greatly interested in the Oder–Neisse frontier, since recognition of it would remove a useful means of bringing the Poles to heel. (That might be a reason for the West to be conciliatory on this point.)

A ban on nuclear weapons for the Bundeswehr seems a more likely aim. But Russian fears about this cannot be taken quite at face value. If the Bundeswehr is to assist in defending Western Europe (including ourselves), it cannot be armed with weapons inferior to those of its potential opponent. The new German army's problem, it has been said, is that it has to be large enough to deter Russia and small enough not to frighten Belgium. Evidently, these conditions are hard to fulfil. It is more logical to oppose German re-armament altogether: (Though the consequences of this – a vast increase in British defence expenditure – were never faced. The Bevanite Left *both* opposed German re-armament *and* increased British expenditure on defence.) Like the British Rhine Army, therefore, the Bundeswehr must be equipped with tactical nuclear weapons. That is the case at present, though the weapons remain under American lock and key. The Russians fear, it is said, German control over these weapons. But it is not clear why the Russians should fear this. The German army could hardly use them to recover the 'lost territories' without losing the territories they hold at present. Those who claim that nuclear weapons in German hands are dangerous are often the same people who argue that nuclear weapons in British hands are ineffective. Why should the Russians be afraid of a German deterrent when they are not afraid of a British? Germany is at least as vulnerable to long-range weapons as Britain, and much more likely to be devastated in a limited nuclear-cum-conventional war. There may be good arguments against letting Germany have nuclear weapons (for example, that it would prejudice reunification). But the Russians canno rationally fear a nuclear Bundeswehr as much as they are said to. In these matters the Russians are realists. More likely, a ban on nuclear weapons would be welcome to them for other reasons. It would demonstrate to the Germans that their allies do not trust them, and thus sow dissension between Germany and the West.

I believe that the recognition of East German sovereignty was very much at the top of Khrushchev's list. Why should this be? It is said that this has become a matter of prestige. But that is to misunderstand the Communist mentality. Communists are not interested in prestige; they are interested in power. Does the thesis that Khrushchev needs East German recognition for reasons of prestige explain the energy Khrushchev expended on the matter between 1958 and 1962? Surely the energy expended is incommensurate with the goal. What is involved, after all, is not an extension of power. In East Germany, Russia has the power. No paper guarantee could secure East Germany's frontiers as effectively as the 400,000 soldiers of the Red Army. Yet the course of the crisis suggested that the other items on the agenda – including West Berlin – were subordinate to this goal. It is necessary to explain this priority. I submit that no explanation will do that does not offer Khrushchev some important potential reward: a reward in terms of an extension of Communist power or a diminution of Western power. What reward of this kind is in sight? The only possible answer, I believe, is Germany itself. Ten years before, Stalin had failed in the struggle for Germany. Yet Germany had remained, during the fifties, despite West German prosperity and the success of Bonn's new democracy, a potentially unstable factor. The division of Germany, though a 'reality', had not been accepted by the German people in East or West. This non-acceptance was also a reality. The contempt of the East Germans for their regime had grown, not decreased, as the decade wore on. The resentment felt by West Germans at Russian division of their country did not diminish.

Yet, paradoxically, Russia is in a position to discount this resentment in her political battle for Germany. The reason is simple: Russia holds the key to German unity. The West is presented with a situation of appalling difficulty. To build a viable Western Europe, she needs West Germany. But West Germany cannot agree to cooperate unless the West pledges itself to work for German reunification. It is true that the West can do little positive in that direction. But she must support the claim of the West German state to be the only legitimate successor to the Reich. What the Western allies are asked to do is therefore something negative; they must not prejudice the chances of a future reunification of Germany in freedom. The Russians hold the key to unity. But the Western allies can never afford to be outbid. They cannot unite Germany by themselves; but they must never surrender the initiative by recognizing Ulbricht's illegitimate, undemocratic, separatist state. The moment they do that, it will be clear to the Germans that the West is not in sympathy with their fundamental aims. This is not a question of sentiment; it is a question of hard national interests. If the West repudiates their interests, what alternative will the Germans have but to turn to the East? Russia will be able to exploit the anti-Western feelings produced by the betrayal, and harness German nationalism to its purpose. Of course, it is in the logic of the situation that the Germans *must* sooner or later turn to Russia if they want to reunify Germany. That is not in dispute. But we must see to it that when they do this they do it in a spirit of loyalty to the West, a spirit that will preserve the work of West European unity and not prejudice our own security. It is because de Gaulle realizes this very well that he refused to conciliate the Russians during the Berlin crisis.

Here, evidently, is a prospect which would justify Khrushchev's offensive. The European front, which had hardened after Stalin's failure in 1949, might be broken up again. The threat of a united, prosperous Europe on Russia's doorstep might still be removed. I believe this prospect alone can explain the offensive that began in November 1958. Khrushchev was not 'preserving the *status quo*'. On the contrary, like Stalin in 1947, he was determined to frustrate the new pattern of European recovery before it was too late. Nor was Khrushchev influenced towards greater reasonableness abroad by his policy of destalinization in Russia and Eastern Europe. On the contrary, he thought it necessary for the Party to regain the political initiative after the hesitations of the Thaw and the troubles in Poland and Hungary. In any case, by exploiting Eastern Europe's anti-Germanism he was able to short-circuit incipient revisionism. That Khrushchev appears to have failed in his offensive is satisfactory. But we must know the reason. Was it British 'flexibility' or German, French, and American 'firmness' that caused him to fail? I have given my own view: it is that the middle course steered by President Kennedy was wise. Nevertheless, I believe that the prospect of further concessions, so far from persuading Khrushchev to end the crisis, decided him to protract it. He had intended to bring the crisis to a head in November 1962. It was not Western conciliatoriness, but the Cuba showdown, that put a temporary end to the offensive.

What was Britain thinking during those months? The British government's public posture, particularly in the speeches of Lord Home, was not less firm than that of its allies. The same cannot be said of public opinion. Let us examine the record. I have spoken of the persistence of anti-Germanism in Britain. In the fifties, this was no more than a curiosity. But, in the context of the Berlin crisis, it became a political factor of some importance. The liking for the Berliners that existed in 1948 had gone. Like the Czechs in 1938, the Berliners were now accused of stubbornness and political incendiarism. In August 1962, an East German boy, Peter Fechter, was shot by Communist police while escaping from East Berlin. Within sight of Allied guards, the boy was permitted to bleed to death. The Communists refused to rescue him themselves, and ordered Western guards and police to keep away. This cruelty was compounded by the folly of the Western authorities. No ambulance was sent (as could easily have been done); an American officer was overheard to say, 'It's not our problem.' It was too much for the nerves of the Berliners. Serious rioting broke out in the city, directed against the Americans as well as the Russians. It was an unfortunate, but humanly understandable incident. Yet, in a *New Statesman* report on 24 August, Mr R. H. S. Crossman could write:

As if they were automata reacting to Ulbricht's unspoken instructions, the West Berliners last week began digging the grave in which, if they have their way, their own liberties will soon be buried. For nearly three years Mr Khrushchev has resisted the East German demand that he should sign a separate peace treaty and start pushing the Western allies out of Berlin – on the ground, apparently, that this policy was fraught with danger and *could be accepted only under grave provocation from the West*. Even in his most optimistic moments, Ulbricht could hardly have expected the West Berliners to make his case for him by demonstrating so violently in their determination to frustrate any peaceful coexistence so long as the presence of Western troops permits them to do so. [My italics.]

Of the Berlin crisis itself, Mr Crossman wrote:

The blunt truth is that the present threat to West Berlin is *almost entirely due to the weakness of Britain and America in conniving at West German and West Berlin attitudes* which must, if much longer tolerated, end in disaster. [My italics.]

Mr Crossman concluded:

Must we really permit a mob of hysterical West Berliners to drag us to the brink of war so that we can start the negotiations under duress which we should have begun of our own accord three years ago? I believe that both President Kennedy and Mr Macmillan have long since realized that the right policy would be to *accept the existence of the two Germanies* and negotiate a settlement based upon it – even if this involved overriding the protests of Bonn and West Berlin. But they can *start the negotiations over the heads of the Germans* only if public opinion is alerted to the danger of drifting into war. [My italics.]

In suggesting that the West negotiate 'over the heads of the Germans', Mr Crossman was not alone. This view was as strongly held on the Right as on the Left. Attacking a Foreign Office pamphlet (price one shilling) *The Meaning of Berlin*, the *Evening Standard* wrote in an editorial on 19 January 1962:

> While President Kennedy is approaching the Berlin problem in the manner promised in his inaugural address – neither negotiating out of fear nor fearing to negotiate – Dr Adenauer must be aware that his demands make a Berlin settlement impossible.
>
> These attitudes are based on a refusal to recognize that the division of Germany, and the 'lost territories' beyond the Oder–Neisse line, are the cost his people must pay for the expensive dictatorship of Hitler.
>
> It is precisely *because Germany is 'large and energetic' that division is sound policy*. That is the essential point about Berlin, and nobody should have to pay a shilling to understand it. [My italics.]

It is clear that British anti-Germanism was regarded, by the Beaverbrook press, as a potent political force. It was freely made use of in the anti-Common-Market campaign. In the *Evening Standard* for 29 January 1962 Mr Willi Frischauer wrote that there existed a

> conspiracy of silence ... designed to make people forget the unpalatable name and personality of the real boss of Brussels, who is neither smooth nor pleasant nor French but a German – none other than Dr Adenauer's old and trusted crony, Professor Walter Hallstein. ... Hallstein, frankly, sees himself as the first president of Europe. Where Hitler failed in war, Hallstein expects to succeed in peace. ...
>
> To Adenauer and Hallstein, however, no economic sacrifice is too great if it helps to bring about an advance towards German-controlled political domination of Europe.

That this pro-Russian, anti-German campaign was conceived and executed with some refinement is suggested by the following juxtaposition (22 August 1962). The *Evening Standard* carried a review by Mr Alexander Werth of a Soviet book on the defenders of Leningrad. This concluded:

It may be asked why the Russians today should publish such potent anti-war books describing the horrors of a war in which they lost 20 million people. Personally I am convinced that Russia (which, unlike Germany, has no territorial claims anywhere) hates war more deeply than any other country, after what she has gone through.

Next to this was printed a reader's letter, in bold type, referring to the recent murder of Peter Fechter at the Wall:

The Germans are capable of protest when one innocent boy is shot down on the Berlin border. Where were their protests when millions were tortured to death in the horror camps in their midst?

The implications of this are plain: because they once tolerated Nazism, the Germans are not deserving of our sympathy now. The ethical implications are horrific. In effect, it is Nazi morality in reverse: where the Nazis once regarded other races as sub-human, the anti-Germans now regard Germans as sub-human. The Teutons are beyond the pale of civilization. Translated into political terms, the effect was to *deny that Britain's treaty obligations to West Germany are binding*. It was at this point that anti-Germanism became a political factor in the Berlin crisis. For anti-Germanism provided appeasement with a moral justification. The attitude was to be found at both ends of the political spectrum. Charon wrote in the *New Statesman*'s London Diary (October 1961):

For one who has a phobia – not, as I think, utterly unfounded – of armed Germans, any attempt to keep Germany disunited has my enthusiastic support. The more walls they build between East and West the safer I feel.

Towards the centre of the spectrum, these sentiments were phrased more circumspectly, but they were not absent. The *Observer* wrote (3 December 1961), concerning an interview recently given to Mr Adshubei by President Kennedy:

The West German government does not oppose negotiations for a new agreement on Berlin: what it fears is the President's hope of living happily ever after. . . . The Federal government . . . while renouncing the use of force, is determined that Europe shall not be allowed to settle down until Germany has been reunited. For that reason it wants to increase its own armed forces and to strengthen Nato. And while Dr Adenauer himself has not asked for nuclear weapons, his Defence Minister, Herr Strauss, is buying missiles . . . which have a nuclear capability, and aircraft . . . which have a nuclear role.

Evidently, it is really the *German* threat with which *Observer* readers ought to be concerned, not the Russian. The Russian aim is to 'preserve the *status quo*'. It is Germany that threatens the peace of Europe. Of sympathy with the Berliners and the East Germans there is little evidence. The cycle of appeasement has run full circle. Once again, it is Czech stubbornness that threatens the peace of Europe, not Hitler's ambitions.

Of course, international politics are not a matter of sentiment. But Britain is the ally of Germany in Nato. Under the Paris Treaties of 1954 Britain had accepted specific political obligations (including the non-recognition of East Germany). More striking than the lack of sympathy was the frivolity with which these solemn obligations were treated. There was no sense of the possible consequences to Britain of treating her partner in this way (such as, in practical terms, Germany's opposition to Britain's entry into the Common Market). Yet the future of Germany was hardly a matter of indifference to Britain. Indeed, the propaganda of the anti-Germans suggested that fear of West Germany had become hysterical. How, then, could commentators regard negotiations 'over the heads of the Germans' with equanimity? It is a strange contradiction. Yet, in speaking of German interests, *The Times* itself set the tone. After a Bonn leakage of American proposals on Berlin, *The Times* wrote (16 April 1962):

It is a little hard to see why the State Department should be quite so much upset at the German leakage of the new American talking points on Berlin. *Of course, the Germans should not have done it. It was irritating of them.* . . . The exact truth about the business is difficult to come by. It may, however, be some consolation to reflect that if the Germans were going to be wildly indignant they would be so in any case, whether they learnt publicly about the proposals before the talks opened or half-way through. *There is something to be said for their getting used to the ideas under discussion.* [My italics.]

To the outsider, the British reaction to the crisis must have seemed well-nigh unanimous: negotiations at all costs, if necessary 'over the heads of the Germans'. This view was expressed more stridently and with greater relish at the ends of the spectrum. But it was found no less in the papers of the centre: *The Times*, the *Guardian*, the *Observer*. It is a pattern with which we are already familiar: the pattern of Cuba Week. But it is the tone in which Germany is spoken of that is significant, not the argument alone. This is evident if we compare the *Times* comment I have quoted with a comparable American voice. In the *Observer* (17 December 1961) Mr MacGeorge Bundy had this to say of the future of the Western alliance, and of Germany's position in it:

We have in prospect, then, a new Europe, with the economic strength, the military self-confidence, and the political unity of a true Great Power. In each of the three areas of traditional analysis, the role of Germany is central. The free men of Germany have accepted the restraints of partnership. In return they have received our pledge of peaceful support for the union of Germany. This was not a hard pledge for us to give. The division of Germany is a mordant sorrow to the Germans and a danger to mankind. It takes no superhuman wisdom to understand the simple truth – a truth beyond cold war rivalries – that *to insist upon the division of Germany is to insist upon a permanent threat to the peace of Europe.* . . . There are ways, we believe, in which the reasonable interests of a reasonable Soviet government can be met – that is why we believe in negotiation. But we can never accept any settlement that undermines the trust, and the commitment to freedom, of the people of the Federal German republic.

Germany is thus a central concern. This does not make Germany all-powerful in the alliance. We cannot grant – and no German statesmen have sought – a German veto on the policy of the West.

A partnership of free men can never move at the call of one member only. But it remains a fundamental purpose of our policy in Europe – and at Berlin – that the free people of Germany shall not have any legitimate cause to regret their trust in us. [My italics.]

The contrast between the tone of this and the tone of most British comment during the crisis hardly needs to be stressed. If the Cuba crisis revealed a hesitant British loyalty to the Americans, the Berlin crisis revealed that the British thought they were still at war with the Germans.

CHAPTER 12

INDIA AND NON-ALIGNMENT

'NON-ALIGNMENT is dead,' I was told, reporting in India shortly after the outbreak of Indo-Chinese hostilities in October 1962. For India it was a moment of great peril. The Indian Army had been routed in the foothills of the Himalayas. Assam, with its oil-wells and tea-estates, lay open to the invader. Nehru's last reservations about accepting military aid from the West were crumbling. In a letter to President Kennedy he had asked, not only for small arms, but for mountain artillery, transport and fighter aircraft, and the men to fly them. Had the Chinese pressed on, the course of events seemed predictable. Non-aligned India would have to invoke American protection. With the U.S. Marines in Calcutta, Bengal might have become a second Korea. India might have become a member of the Western alliance; Pakistan, not to be outdone, might have declared herself non-aligned. In the upshot, none of this took place. Why? Did Russia intervene on India's behalf? Did the 'moral pressure' of world opinion persuade China to turn back? These factors may have been at work, though Indians have exaggerated their importance. I think rather that the Chinese feared a repetition of the Korean situation. Given Soviet neutrality, a Korea-type Western task force would quickly have restored the balance. Probably the Chinese were well aware of this. They called off their invasion before it reached the point of diminishing returns.

'Non-alignment is dead.' But is non-alignment dead? How has India's experience affected Indonesia, Ghana, and Ceylon? Has non-alignment survived the onslaught on

India, which did more than any other nation to originate and foster the concept? The truth I fear, is, that non-alignment has survived very well. Six months have passed and non-alignment is not dead. The show goes on; India no longer takes part. Indeed, what has happened is what China may have intended to happen. India's prestige as the leading exponent of non-alignment has gone. She has lost her innocence. Her old friends avoid her company. Why? It seems a strange result. If a member of the non-aligned club is threatened, surely fellow-members will rush to her defence? Yet that is not at all what has happened. Why? I am not imputing motives of cowardice to India's former friends. On certain issues, the non-aligned nations have shown that they can stand up to Russian and American pressure (the *troika* solution for the U.N. secretariat was successfully resisted). That India's friends have deserted her has a different motive. Their behaviour is dictated, I believe, by the very logic of non-alignment. After hostilities had begun, Dr Nkrumah sent a telegram to Mr Macmillan begging him not to 'aggravate the situation' by sending arms '*to either side*' [my italics]. At the Colombo conference of non-aligned powers in December, Ceylon, Burma, Indonesia, and Ghana were careful not to commit themselves to one side or the other. To have done so, they said, would have cast doubt on their neutrality and compromised the peace mission they intended to send to Peking. Privately, they expressed sympathy with India. Publicly, as non-aligned powers, they observed a strict neutrality between New Delhi and Peking.

The same process can be seen at work in the reactions of British neutralists. In the past, India had enjoyed enormous prestige among them for her championship of non-alignment. Yet no sooner had India been attacked by China than her neutralist admirers withdrew their support. Thus Lord Russell, in his *Unarmed Victory* (April 1963), has written that though in the past

the Indian government stood in general for peace and conciliation ... there was evidence ... that when India's national interests were involved, the Indian government was not capable of the impartiality which it urged in disputes to which it was not a party. The chief instances of this were Kashmir and Nagaland . . .

If India's past reputation is not unblemished, the present charge against her is grave:

Already, India has ceased, in fact though not in form, to be neutral as between East and West, and has, thereby, *increased the chance of world war*. [My italics.]

In the eyes of Western neutralists, of course, India's offence is to have turned to the West for arms. Interestingly, those nations – like Indonesia and Egypt – which have turned to Russia and China for arms are not considered to have 'increased the chance of world war'.

. . . it cannot be wholly pleasant for Communist powers to have India turn entirely to the West in spite of the fact that Russia has been friendly to her. But perhaps the worst blow to the peace of the world is the fact that her defection from strict non-alignment weakens the block of neutral powers and their potential weight as arbitrators, especially since India was more politically mature than most of the others and has been regarded as a leader in all matters where neutrality might be helpful.

Initially, Lord Russell's reaction had been favourable to the Indian case:

When fighting began in the disputed regions, I thought at first, as did almost everybody in the West, that China was wholly in the wrong and had undoubtedly been the aggressor.

Lord Russell proceeds to argue that the *facts* of the case are secondary – it is the preservation of peace that matters.

From the point of view of the rest of the world and of humanity in general the details of the boundary dispute are irrelevant. What is clear is that there ought not to be war over them. The Chinese ceasefire and withdrawal strongly suggest that China is more anxious to put an end to the conflict than is India.

It is a staggering reversal. How does Lord Russell, initially pro-Indian, arrive at this new assessment? At the beginning of November, a few days after the first Chinese onslaught, Lord Russell had sent a telegram to Prime Minister Nehru. Nehru had replied:

Thank you for your telegram dated 8 November. Chou En-lai's offer of a cease-fire on the basis of the Chinese three-point proposal is in effect a demand for surrender on terms to be accepted and implemented while large Chinese armies are on Indian soil. No country, much less India, can submit to the military dictates of an aggressor.

We have no desire to continue military conflict, nor do we desire any part of Chinese territory, but there can be no compromise with aggression. The first essential if we are to revert to peaceful processes is to undo the aggression by restoring the *status quo ante* 8 September 1962.   Jawaharlal Nehru

Lord Russell comments:

Both in tone and in substance this response surprised and distressed me. It held out no hope that any peaceful solution might ever be arrived at, but appeared to be an ultimatum that the Chinese must give in at every point. Though I still thought, and continued for some time to think, that India was the injured party, and my sympathies in this dispute were with her, I was disturbed by the rapidly increasing war hysteria there as evidenced, not only by the tone of this telegram, but by the news given us daily in our press.

Apparently Lord Russell had by now convinced himself that it was the *Indians* who were presenting the *Chinese* with an ultimatum:

The press in this country had waxed almost as hysterical as the Indians themselves in anger against Chinese 'aggression' and, sympathetic as I still was to the Indian point of view, I deeply deplored that the Chinese case should never be presented, for even then. I saw that the Chinese *clearly had a case, whether one agreed or not*. [My italics.]

The verbal evasiveness of this last sentence is significant. After all, 'to have a case' signifies in normal usage not the statement of a position, but a judgement of the correctness of that position. If the Chinese are even partly right, they may be said 'to have a case'. But by saying that the Chinese 'clearly had a case', Lord Russell has actually prejudged the issue, while ostensibly – by using the phrase 'whether one agreed or not' – taking up a neutral position. Yet the confusion is interesting. It is the mark of the neutralist that, for all his moral passion, he frequently refuses to face the moral issue. Lord Russell employs here, and in the following passage, a kind of semantic neutralism. He has already stated that 'the details of the boundary dispute are irrelevant'. Yet he can write, without sense of contradiction:

When populations have been worked up to a pitch of bellicose excitement it becomes very difficult for governments to restrain them. This has happened most notably in India. The government misled the population by concealing the fact that the Chinese had a legal case which, *on the face of it, was as strong as the Indian case,* and that what was needed was negotiation, supplemented by arbitration if necessary. China was willing to adopt this course, but India was not . . . [My italics.]

It is, indeed, a strange reversal. Lord Russell is himself surprised where his logic has led him:

When the Communist revolution took place in China, I felt desolated, though I saw nothing good to uphold in Chiang Kai-shek. I thought that the brainwashing of which I read and the intensive destruction of old traditions and learning would destroy what I found delightful and admirable in China. Now, after the last month, I do not feel at all sure of this.

Lord Russell insists that he is no admirer of Mao's brand of communism:

I both fear and intensely dislike Chinese communism, wherever it differs with the policy of Mr Khrushchev.

Nevertheless, Lord Russell has come round to the view that

. . . China alone had offered to behave reasonably in the lamentable circumstances then obtaining.

Again, the semantic neutralism of these words is worth pondering: there is no talk of an initiator of conflict, only of 'circumstances obtaining'. After the announcement of the ceasefire, Lord Russell issued this statement to the press:

> The announcement by Prime Minister Chou En-lai and the government of China of unilateral ceasefire should be universally welcomed as a generous act. The world was again on the brink of disaster, and only the unimaginative will cavil at congratulating the Chinese for their decision.

Like Mr Khrushchev's action in the Cuban crisis, the Chinese decision is hailed as 'a triumph for unilateralism'.

> I cannot think of any other instance in which a victorious army has been halted in this way by its own government. Because it had seemed to me from Chou En-lai's letter and from my talk with the Chinese Chargé d'Affaires, that the Chinese were, in the matter of the border dispute, reasonable and temperate, I thought it worthwhile to write to Chou En-lai . . . appealing for such magnanimous action on the part of the Chinese government, but I was taken by surprise, as was the rest of the world, that they believed sufficiently clearly and strongly that war must be avoided, to take such extreme measures to make such a sacrifice of their gains.

A month before, at the close of Cuba Week, Lord Russell had written to Mr Khrushchev in the following terms:

My dear Mr Khrushchev,

> I should like you to know of my personal feeling about your solving the Cuban crisis. I have never known any statesman act with the magnanimity and greatness that you have shown over Cuba, and I wish you to be clear that every sincere and honest human being pays you homage for your courage.
>
> With lasting esteem,
>
> Bertrand Russell

He was now to address Mr Khrushchev's Chinese rivals in scarcely less fulsome vein:

Dear Mr Chou En-lai,

> Your letter to me of 24 November has given me the greatest pleasure and I am honoured to receive it. I should wish you to know that your decision not only to withdraw to the lines behind

the positions of 8 September, but to do so unilaterally, fills me with admiration . . .

Lord Russell draws this conclusion from the two great crises of the autumn of 1962:

. . . whenever the question of peace or war is relevant, *the merits of either side become insignificant* in comparison with the importance of peace. In the nuclear age, the human race cannot survive without peace. For this reason, *I shall always side with the more peaceful party* in any dispute between powerful nations. It has happened that in both the disputes . . . the Communist side has been the less bellicose. [My italics.]

I can find no fitter comment on these remarks than a passage from a letter Lord Russell himself quotes. It is from an Indian admirer, bewildered at the logic of the great philosopher:

It is strange, Sir, that a man of your ability and understanding has uttered not a single word to condemn this unprovoked Chinese invasion, and it is further very surprising that you have uttered not a single word of sympathy for India who is a victim of this aggression. I feel you must be misinformed about the true facts of the case, or perhaps great is the philosophy of great persons which a common man fails to understand. If I be wrong to infer like this, I shall be too pleased to know it.

Lord Russell's correspondent was not alone in his bewilderment. I know, from my own observations in India at the time, that many Indians were bitter about their 'betrayal' by neutralist opinion, both in Britain and in the non-aligned world. Of course, it was not tactful to remind them that this had been India's own posture for a decade and a half. However, that is all over and done with. We are concerned here with the present, not with the past. The Indo-Chinese conflict is of interest to us for the light it throws on the practice and morality of non-alignment. Thus, it is evident that non-alignment is not the same thing as 'collective security'. The 'Afro-Asian bloc' has received enormous publicity. Because of that, many people have mistaken it for a conventional political alliance. At times, under the auspices of the United Nations, an Afro-Asian political alliance has momentarily come into being. But the solidarity of the Afro-Asian bloc is rather more intangible. This is not surprising. After all, the nations of the bloc have little in common but the wish to be left alone. They are too far apart geographically (or, where they have territorial claims on one another, too close) to form an effective alliance. But if they wish to be left alone by the great powers, they also wish to receive aid from them. They are in competition for the favour of the great. Thus the non-aligned posture is more contradictory than it appears at first sight. In the past, India maintained that non-alignment was morally superior to commitment to one of the 'Cold War blocs'. What assumptions underlay this attitude? They were certainly not unattractive. Indians thought of the Cold War as a disturbance of the natural pattern of international relations. The natural pattern was represented by the relations existing between the non-aligned powers. Their aim was to extend this area of sanity and non-alignment, mobilizing world opinion through the United Nations, until the Cold War was extinguished for lack of fuel. Non-alignment was not mere neutrality. It was not thought of as a negative thing, but as the model for the harmonious world society of the future.

It was a noble vision. But it rested on a cavalier treatment of the facts of power. Because East and West competed for their favours, the Cold War seemed to the non-aligned a performance put on for their benefit. Let America and Russia fight it out: let us, the non-aligned powers, be the arbiters. But that is too masculine an analogy. Arbitration implies authority and power of enforcement. This the non-aligned powers lacked. They were being wooed. In the competition for the favours of the great they took the woman's part. This is clear if we take the argument *ad absurdum*. If the Cold War ended tomorrow, would the non-aligned powers stand to benefit? Of course, they would share in the general relief. But they would also stand to lose a great deal.

Indeed, they would stand to lose more than the countries that could then cut back their armaments and raise their standard of living. Would Russia and the West be so eager to finance dams, build steel-works, provide free education, once the element of Cold War competition fell away? Plainly, they would not. And, if the economic loss would be severe, the decline in political prestige would be no less so. Who would listen to all those well-meaning, interminable harangues from newly independent statesmen, giving their elders lessons in international deportment? What would become of the artificial structure of Afro-Asian solidarity? Would it not fall like a house of cards? I do not say this in mockery of the new nations. It is right that they should exercise their independence. But there is an element of pretension in their claims to be arbiters between the great powers. And this would very quickly be exposed. The truth is, non-alignment cannot confer powers of arbitration in the Cold War, for non-alignment is itself parasitic on the Cold War.

The morality of non-alignment is ambiguous. A judge, an arbiter, must be the repository of wisdom, impartiality, and justice. We do not think well of a judge who takes bribes, even if he takes them impartially from both sides. Yet that is the invidious situation of the non-aligned countries. Again, is there not a contradiction between the role of arbiter and the neutrality to which the non-aligned statesman is pledged? As an arbiter, he must choose the good. As a neutral, he can have no opinion. Is there not a contradiction, too, between the expectation of aid and the demand for non-interference? I am not arguing against aid; I believe we should give more. But the morality of non-alignment is ambiguous. The non-aligned country is like the sixteen-year-old who will take no advice from his father, yet expects his weekly ten-bob's worth of pocket-money. Father may be generous; but pocket-money and independence do not go well together. Ideologically, too, the non-aligned posture is ambiguous. Though political neutrality does not require ideological neutrality (as Switzerland, Yugoslavia, and Nehru's India show), non-aligned intellectuals frequently recommend it. The non-aligned world wants neither 'capitalism' nor 'socialism'. The Cold War has no moral significance. It is merely a struggle for power. This non-aligned view, it is said, is morally superior to participation in the Cold War. Yet the view itself smacks of indifferentism. Is there really *nothing* to choose between East and West? And indifferentism cannot be presented as a superior moral attitude.

These are not sophistries. In India, propaganda for non-alignment has seriously confused the public mind. Western democracy and Eastern socialism are both said 'to have their good side'. So, perhaps, they have. But India herself is a Western-style democracy. She is justly proud of it. There is no doubt at all where she stands. Yet the indifferentism to which non-alignment gave rise often blunted India's moral discrimination: for example, over Hungary and Tibet. The practical implications of non-alignment, too, were sharply brought home to India by Dr Nkrumah's message to Mr Macmillan, and by the attitude of the Colombo powers. Dr Nkrumah demanded that no arms should be sent 'to either side'. The Colombo powers refused to discriminate between the merits of the Indian and the Chinese cases. To invaded India, of course, this did not seem a moral attitude. Yet it lay in the logic of non-alignment. An alliance for collective security, concerned to restore the balance of power, might have added its weight to India's, and threatened to intervene. Whether this would have been effective one may doubt. But non-alignment is not collective security. The essence of non-alignment is to mediate between the existing power blocs, not to set up a new power bloc. Thus it is inevitable that, in any given conflict, the non-aligned powers should take up *a median position*. Further, they will seek a median position between the adversaries (as did Lord Russell), *not on the merits of the case, but irrespective of them*.

For India, the implications have been painful. India's

'non-alignment', as formerly understood, has vanished overnight. But just as the strength of non-alignment is not the sum of its members, so the subtraction of a member – even if, as in India's case, the most powerful member – does not destroy it. The factors making for the non-alignment of Ghana or Ceylon still operate, and will continue to operate. India will drag her feet, or drop out altogether. Yet India's may prove a general lesson. I do not mean that non-alignment has now been exposed, and should be condemned as foolish and immoral. Its morality is certainly ambiguous; but its practical uses, both to the West and to the non-aligned powers themselves, are still considerable. The non-aligned powers seek to fend off the advances of East and West impartially. By doing so, they are in theory – and sometimes, as Egypt has shown, in practice – helping to resist Communist pressure. Nor is the fact that they receive Soviet aid necessarily against Western interests. Economic success is likely to cement the *status quo* and frustrate violent revolution. On this we may agree with the Chinese rather than with the Russians.

Nevertheless, the logic of the median position does not normally favour the West. There is something incurably feminine in the non-aligned posture. Attempts to 'influence' the non-aligned powers in our favour may be repulsed, not because our influence is evil, but because influence of any kind is resented. Indeed, to save themselves from our embraces, the logic of the median position may cause non-aligned powers to move in the opposite direction – irrespective of the merits of the case. They would like to agree with us; but they have contracted to meet the devil half-way. Again, paradoxically, the very intransigence of the Communists may work in their favour. For the non-aligned are readier to protest against the misdemeanors of the West, which is known to be open to protest, than against Communist troublemaking. This was evident when the Russians broke the test-ban treaty before the opening of the Belgrade Conference of non-aligned powers in September 1961. The

assembled powers failed to protest for fear of aligning themselves with the West. But later protests at American testing
showed that the same reservations did not apply to the more
susceptible West. Thus, as India has discovered, the logic
of the median position *favours the aggressor*. This is especially so where the aggressor is known for his ruthlessness and
the victim for his moral sensitivity – so much is clear from
Lord Russell's account. The point is not that the neutralists
and the non-aligned are a bunch of hypocritical cowards. It is
that the structure of non-alignment, like the structure of the
United Nations, is not made to withstand extreme political
pressures. If they are brought to bear, the structure will
collapse.

Perhaps it was a mistake for the non-aligned powers to
present their case in moral terms. By doing so, they involved
themselves in too many contradictions. They made of the
negative concept of neutrality a positive moral doctrine.
The older European neutrals, such as Sweden and Switzerland, would probably not have made this mistake. During
the war, Swiss neutrality had its uses. But Swiss intellectuals
are still uneasy about their country's neutrality in the
struggle against Hitler. By making too great a virtue of their
neutrality, non-aligned statesmen and intellectuals lost sight
of their starting point. They began to equate the 'pressures
of world opinion', which they could manipulate at the
United Nations, with the balance of power in the East–West
conflict. They were tempted to inflate their political prestige
in this way. The danger is evident. By permitting this in-
flation, non-alignment lost touch with reality and began to
sound pretentious and hypocritical. Realization of this is
now widespread in India. Indeed, there is a strong tendency
to reject non-alignment out of hand. This is understandable,
but unjust. The roots of non-alignment lie in the doctrine of
sovereignty. A new nation is rightly jealous of the sovereignty it has fought for. It is determined to defend it against
all comers. It is acutely sensitive to pressure from outside.
Where an older nation might accept the restraints of an

alliance, the new nation wishes to preserve its freedom of action. Perhaps this is unwise, but it is not dishonourable. What the protagonist of non-alignment is asserting is his sovereign freedom of action – against both the Communists and ourselves. But freedom of action has a corollary: there must be the power to maintain it. If the new nation renounces political and military alliances, it must provide for its defence by other means. Its neutrality must be, like that of Sweden and Switzerland, a 'strong' neutrality. It is often said that the first priority for the new nations must be economic development, not 'useless' military expenditure. That is what the Indian supporters of Mr Krishna Menon now say. But if a nation is not ready to defend herself, it is arguable that she is not ready for sovereignty. If she cannot afford the one, she cannot afford the other.

Stripped of its moral accretions, non-alignment is seen to have been a calculation. India miscalculated. She imagined herself immune from the processes of power-politics. She awoke to find herself in the centre of the maelstrom. Her future course is a severely practical matter. Can she count on Soviet neutrality for the foreseeable future? Can she get arms quickly enough to deter a second onslaught? What long-term measures must she take to contain Chinese expansion and to prevent Chinese hegemony in Asia? What were the origins of her miscalculation? On what did India base her illusions of immunity? The answer is to be found, I believe, in the history of Congress. Congress's enemy was the British Raj; it never reckoned with the possibility of an external threat to India. This was not surprising; the Himalayas seemed an impassable barrier. The British Indian Army was looked upon as an instrument of repression (which it partly was), and not as the guarantee of India's integrity. When the ineffectiveness of that guarantee became evident, after the fall of Singapore and Rangoon, Nehru wanted to assist in India's defence. Gandhi overruled him, and launched his Quit India campaign. The language in which he justified this campaign is of some interest: it is the language of Bertrand Russell and the English pacifists of the thirties:

> If the British left India to her fate as they had to leave Singapore, non-violent India would not lose anything. Probably, the Japanese would leave India alone. Perhaps India would be able effectively to help China in the way of peace and in the long run even play a decisive part in the promotion of world peace.

Indian nationalists cannot be blamed for being anti-British. But they can be blamed for being pro-Japanese. From the experience of China in the preceding decade, they ought to have known what Japanese militarism meant. The Indian Army, of course, fought against Fascism on many battle-fronts. But after Independence it was the leaders of Congress who made India's foreign policy. Congress leaders looked on the army they had inherited as a relic of British imperialism. They were not likely to ask its advice. It is not surprising, therefore, that the attitudes Congress displayed in 1942 dominated the first years of Indian independence.

Congress complacency towards the Japanese threat was equalled by its post-war complacency towards the growth of Chinese power. During the two centuries of British rule, China had been too weak to constitute a threat. The buffer states Britain set up on the borders of her Indian Empire – Nepal, Tibet, Afghanistan, a sphere of influence in southern Persia – were designed as a check to Russian rather than Chinese imperialism. Traditionally, the invaders of the sub-continent – Aryans, Greeks, Huns, Moghuls – had entered India from the north-west. The Himalayas were an effective barrier against Chinese ambitions. Again, cultural influences had always been from west to east. China, Japan, south-east Asia adopted Indian Buddhism; India remained scarcely less ignorant of Chinese civilization than Europe. To some extent, these historical memories lay behind the obsession with Pakistan, and the blindness to China, that marked Indian policy after Independence. To be fair to the politicians, the army seems also to have discounted a Chinese threat. It had been trained by the British, so the notion of a Chinese invasion across the Himalayas was not easily entertained. But there were deeper reasons for Nehru's blindness towards China. It was recognized that Mao Tse-tung had restored China, potentially, to the ranks of the great powers. In 1949 this was seen as a triumph for Asian nationalism. Chiang Kai-shek was dropped by Nehru with almost indecent haste. Mao's Communist militancy seemed to constitute no threat. Indeed, it was the other way about. Because China's power had been restored under Communist auspices India's leaders were reassured. Military unrealism, the legacy of Gandhism, was compounded by illusions about the nature of communism.

The source of these illusions is not difficult to guess at. The reader of Nehru's *Autobiography* comes upon many passages such as this:

> So I turned inevitably with good will towards communism, for, whatever its faults, it was at least not hypocritical and not imperialistic. It was not a doctrinal adherence, as I did not know much about the finer points of communism, my acquaintance being limited at the time to its broad features. . . . With all her blunders, Soviet Russia had triumphed over enormous difficulties, and taken great strides towards this new order. While the rest of the world was in the grip of the depression and going backward in some ways, in the Soviet Union a great new world was being built up before our eyes.

Nehru wrote these words in prison in 1934. Again, the sentiments were those current on the British Left at the time. Nehru is hardly to be blamed for thinking well of Soviet Russia. He had little reason to love British imperialism. Communism seemed an attractive alternative. Unlike Cole, Laski, Strachey, and the Webbs, he had not had the opportunity to study this alternative. But Nehru's views would not have mattered if they had not survived into the fifties and become the views of a great part of the Indian intelligentsia. Why did they survive? The answer, again, is to be found in Indian experience. As India was shielded from the impact of militant Fascism in the thirties, so she was shielded from the impact of militant communism in the forties. These years saw India preoccupied with the problems of Partition and her new-found Independence. Europe's disillusionment with communism, which set in at the end of the war, passed the Indian intelligentsia by. Neither the rape of Czechoslovakia, nor the Berlin blockade, nor the Korean aggression made any impact in India. There, the ideas of the English thirties, disseminated by the Left Book Club and the *New Statesman*, survived the period of English disillusionment and lived on into the fifties. It was these ideas that justified Nehru's appeasement of China. (Though China's espousal of peaceful coexistence also convinced many in the West. It was customary to emphasize the 'Chineseness' of Chinese communism, and contrast it with the rigid dogmatism of Russian communism.) Nor was it only in India that these ideas lived on. The worst harm done by the Russian illusions of the English thirties was not done in England at all. The chief victims were the ex-colonial countries. To us, Victor Gollancz's Left Book Club, Kingsley Martin's *New Statesman*, Harold Laski's London School of Economics, may be vanished glories. To many ex-colonial intellectuals they are still the Light of Asia.

Britain's posthumous political influence, then, has been remarkable. But what can Britain do today? The autumn crisis of 1962 showed that a fund of good will towards the West – and particularly towards Britain – still exists in India. Indeed, it became evident that the non-aligned world, however it may protest at specific Western actions, expects the West to assist it in emergencies. How can this good will towards Britain be mobilized? More concretely, what can Britain contribute to prevent a fresh invasion? Inevitably, the aid Britain can give is more limited than that of the United States. The task that faces India is to reassume the responsibilities of the Indian Empire. Here, Britain and the Commonwealth may be in a position to help with advice, information, and political support. (The warmth of the Indian response, of course, is not unconnected with that decline in British power which has removed us as a potential threat. And this is a point of general application. Where America is feared because she is strong – as in Latin America – Britain's weakness may be a source of political strength. Equally, the lack of cohesion in the Western alliance, which was so grave a weakness in the Berlin crisis, may be a source of Western strength. Britain's role as the minor partner in the Anglo-American alliance need not always be negative.)

What, then, were the responsibilities of British power in India? They were twofold: central and peripheral. The central responsibility was to secure the sub-continent against territorial encroachment. The protective girdle of buffer-states sprang from this responsibility. British India was not a geopolitical vacuum, as Congress assumed, seeing in the Indian Army only an instrument of repression. The Indian Army was the strongest military force between China (and later Japan) in the east, the Ottoman Empire in the west, and the Russian Empire in the north. It is true that none of these powers ever challenged the British hold on India. But the existence of a powerful Indian Army was a strong deterrent. The peripheral responsibility of British power in India was to secure the Indian Ocean. It was by the sea-routes that Britain had conquered India; their security was vital to the survival of the Raj. No power could be allowed to establish a base in the Indian Ocean and threaten India's trade and communications. A chain of bases was built from Capetown, through East Africa, Aden, southern Persia, Burma, Malaya, Singapore, to British Australasia. Many of these bases came under the Viceroy at New Delhi. In protecting them India protected herself.

How have India's defence prospects changed since British days? Certainly, they have not changed for the better. India's strategic interests are what they always were: the defence of the sub-continent and of the sea-routes. But the Indian Empire is now split into five territorial units: India, East and West Pakistan, Burma, and Ceylon. The protective girdle to the north has been pierced by the

Chinese in Tibet, and is endangered in Nepal, Bhutan, and Sikkim. The bases around the Indian Ocean are still for the most part in Commonwealth hands. But their long-term continuance is in jeopardy. Chinese or Russian control of a base in the Indian Ocean would confront India, without the Royal Navy to protect her, with a serious threat. British power in India was never challenged in a military sense, except by Japan in its last days. But Russia and China, the two great land-powers to the north, are stronger now than they were in the entire history of the British Raj. In view of these changes, all of them to India's disadvantage, it is no wonder that New Delhi gave economics preference over strategy. Yet Indian opinion is aware that this order of priorities may have to be reversed. The danger of Communist infiltration in Burma and Ceylon, and perhaps elsewhere on the borders of the Indian Ocean, is clearly growing. India is now ready to accept Western aid, and this will be forthcoming. For the West, almost any sacrifice should be worthwhile to preserve India as a democratic state. If the military efforts that India must make threaten her economic progress, the West must see that financial aid, if necessary on a massive scale, is made available to her.

Economically, if aid continues to flow, the problem of 'take-off' should be solved within the next decade. India's planning targets are laid down. If growth is less rapid than in China and Russia, mistakes on the scale of Stalin's collectivization or of Mao's Great Leap Forward are unlikely. Militarily, the position is more sombre. India must arrive at an estimate of Communist intentions. Can she depend on Soviet neutrality? How soon will China acquire nuclear weapons? What should India's reaction be? Here, non-alignment becomes relevant once again. For India to regard *both* Communist powers as potential enemies could have only one consequence: she would have to align herself with the West and seek shelter under the West's nuclear umbrella. This may well be what China wants. But it does not appear to be what Russia wants. There is reason to think that Russia will wish to limit India's alignment with the West by an attitude of benevolent neutrality. It seems that India can speculate on Sino-Soviet rivalries to this extent: it is as important to Russia to prevent the complete domination of India by China as it is important to Russia to prevent the complete domination of India by the West. This does not mean that India can expect Russia to supply her with massive military aid: that would be too open a challenge to China. But it may mean that the Soviet Union will tolerate Western military aid in the interests of containing China. Non-alignment is here a matter of calculation. But the calculation is probably sound enough for the immediate future. India should regard China as the main threat, and remain 'non-aligned' towards Russia and the West.

There remains the question of nuclear weapons. It is certain that China will have them within the next few years, if she does not have them already. These weapons will be of no military significance for the first decade of their existence as a deterrent to the major nuclear powers. But nuclear weapons of even the most primitive variety in the hands of China would have a remarkable psychological effect in Asia. What was no threat to America or Russia would seem a terrifying threat to China's non-nuclear neighbours. Already, the brief triumph of Chinese arms in India has encouraged her smaller neighbours to seek reassurance in Peking. If China becomes a nuclear power, what should India do? The choices before her would seem to be these. She could slip under the American nuclear umbrella. She would then be as fully 'aligned' as those Asian clients of America on whom she has poured the vials of her contempt: Pakistan, Siam, Chiang Kai-shek, Syngman Rhee. Nor would the Russians continue their policy of benevolent neutrality.

An alternative might be to appeal to one of the smaller nuclear powers for help – for example, to Britain. This would have certain advantages. If the British V-bombers will soon be no deterrent to Russia, they will long remain a deterrent to China. Conceivably, this could provide Britain's nuclear arsenal with a new lease of life. For a deterrent that is a threat to China but is not a threat to the Soviet Union is what India requires in her peculiar political circumstances. The third choice would be for India to match, bomb for bomb, China's growing nuclear force. This would be very much more expensive; but it would be technically feasible. India's choice is painfully difficult. She is being asked to reassume the responsibilities Britain once bore, at a time when the constellation of forces has moved greatly to her disadvantage. I have said that the positive content of non-alignment was freedom of action. Whatever happens, India must strive to retain her freedom of action as a sovereign state – against ourselves, her friends, as well as against her potential enemies. If the pressure grows too great, there is the risk, in India as in other newly independent countries, that sovereignty painfully acquired may again be lost. Paradoxically, it is Britain's task to help India preserve what India once compelled Britain to surrender.

CHAPTER 13
GREAT WARS, LITTLE WARS

In an earlier chapter, we discussed the prospects for liberalization in the countries of the Communist bloc. We concluded that there was no certain correlation between greater liberty at home and greater reasonableness abroad. The analogy with imperialist Europe before 1914 was not encouraging. Perhaps that was too abstract an approach. Yet examination of the record confirmed it. It is true that Stalin's offensive coincided with a fresh assault on intellectual freedom in Russia and Eastern Europe. But the strategic reversal that followed – the policy of peaceful coexistence – was not the product of liberalization. The policy was originated by Stalin, after the failure of the 1947–52 offensive. It is true that Malenkov's – and later Khrushchev's and Bulganin's – preaching of peaceful coexistence coincided with destalinization in the Soviet Union and that this increased the doctrine's attractiveness. But the return to a more aggressive foreign policy in 1958, though heralded by a tightening of the reins, did not plunge Russia back to the terror of the *Yezhovshchina* of the thirties, or the *Zhdanovshchina* of the forties. Internal liberalization – in the limited sense of 'rationalization' or *embourgeoisement* – has been fairly steady since Stalin's death. Russia's growing industrial sophistication, her new sense of invulnerability, her educational advances, have all played their part. But this has not made her posture in the world less aggressive. The most violent phase of destalinization – the 22nd Congress in October 1961, in the course of which Stalin was removed from the Lenin Mausoleum – coincided with a phase of extreme Soviet aggressiveness over Berlin, with threats against Scandinavia, and with the resumption of nuclear testing. The 1962 anti-Stalinist, anti-dogmatist, anti-Chinese campaign coincided with the preparation of the Cuba coup. If Khrushchev has temporarily abandoned his offensive, it is not because Russia has become more liberal. It is because the West has made credible its will to resist his encroachments.

During recent crises, some have argued that we ought to conciliate Khrushchev in order to make his task easier at home. Khrushchev, it is said, is our best bet; we must not let the 'Stalinists' return to power. But is it our business to be concerned for Khrushchev's position? Is it so certain that we should be worse off with his successor? Before Khrushchev's accession, it was Malenkov who was considered the liberal. Malenkov favoured more consumer goods; Khrushchev stood for 'Stalinist' orthodoxy. Yet no sooner had Khrushchev removed Malenkov from power than he adopted his policies. I believe the case is instructive. The external policies of the Kremlin are dictated by the facts of the world situation, not by the whims of particular Soviet leaders. The distinction Western journalists draw between 'liberals' and 'Stalinists' in the Kremlin is largely imaginary. I have even read – in an *Evening Standard* editorial – about a 'pro-Western group in the Kremlin'. But there is no more a pro-Western group in the Kremlin than there is a pro-Kremlin group in the British Cabinet. The men in the Kremlin are not our friends.

Internal liberalization will continue whoever leads the Soviet Union. It is a welcome process. But it is probably not one we can consciously influence. Unconsciously, of course, we do exert a liberalizing influence in Eastern Europe through our jazz, our fashions, our films, our books, our newspapers. Without this constant pressure, liberalization would proceed at a very different pace. But this is a battle we are winning – as any visitor to Poland or Hungary knows – without conscious effort. Indeed conscious effort, by putting the Soviets on their guard, might retard the process. What the West *can* influence is the external behaviour of the Soviet Union and of China. But here we cannot rely on evolutionary forces to do our work for us. The same forces that are liberalizing the Soviet Union are also making her stronger. It was the growing strength of the Soviet Union that encouraged Khrushchev to launch his offensive in 1958. The only real influence we can exert on the Soviet Union and China is that of countervailing power. The only sure equation is that Communist aggressiveness is in inverse proportion to the weakness, disunity, and passivity of the West. That is the lesson of the Berlin blockade, of Korea, of Cuba Week. We are sometimes told that we ought not do this or that because 'it might provoke the Communists'. But totalitarians are not such sensitive plants. This was the mistake Geoffrey Dawson made when he fought to keep out of *The Times* anything that might offend Nazi susceptibilities. Totalitarians know only one provocation: weakness.

Thermo-nuclear weapons have made all-out war as unacceptable to the Communists as it is to the West. But though the nuclear stalemate has made war more unlikely, it has not made it impossible. It has not ensured stability. Nor will it do so as long as two blocs with radically conflicting interests and ideologies confront one another. I have argued that the most stable solution – a world authority based on a condominium of the two super-powers – is impossible as long as the Communists mean by peaceful coexistence what we understand by Cold War. If the Communists could really 'accept the *status quo*', as Mr Crankshaw and Mr Deutscher suggest, such a condominium would be possible. Then, indeed, 'communism would no longer be communism'. But the evidence I have assembled in these chapters does not point to a 'withering away' of Marxism–Leninism. The chances of a condominium are therefore poor. The nuclear stalemate has created a certain community of interest between the two blocs. Yet it has not prevented the most bitter political conflicts between them. This is not, of course, in contradiction with the Communist interpretation of peaceful coexistence. I do not think primarily of the Chinese invasion of India. That was, in a sense, anomalous. If the Chinese had pressed on, a Korean situation would have developed in Assam. In relation to China, India was still in a pre-Korean situation. To China, India was that intolerable provocation: a power vacuum. Had the Chinese pressed on, that vacuum would quickly have been filled.

This does not mean that conventional warfare is impossible in the nuclear age. America, after all, was a nuclear power at the time of Korea. On the contrary, as a result of the nuclear stalemate, conventional strategy has come into its own again. That is why it is vital to increase Europe's conventional capacity. At present, the West would have to be the first to resort to nuclear weapons if attacked. Yet the inhibitions the West would experience in being the first to use nuclear weapons are very great. Thus Soviet conventional superiority gives her not only a physical but a psychological advantage. (Practical opponents of nuclear warfare should perhaps be demonstrating for the reintroduction of conscription.) Nevertheless, the Korean experience has not been forgotten in Moscow and Peking. If she were so inclined, the Soviet Union could overrun Persia and the Middle East tomorrow. There might or might not be a Western nuclear response. But the West could not afford to see the Middle East pass into Soviet hands. A prolonged conventional struggle would ensue. But this would lead either to all-out nuclear war or to the same inconclusive result as in Korea. A conventional smash-and-grab raid – such as China attempted in India – is not a tempting prospect for the Soviet Union while the West remains on the alert.

It is more likely that the Soviets will use their nuclear-cum-conventional power to wage a war of nerves against the Western alliance, exploiting the divisions between its members. That is why, during the Berlin crisis, the Communists did what they could to foster anti-German feeling in Britain and America (in Germany they fostered anti-American and anti-British feeling). Indeed, the existence of these divisions was an important factor in Khrushchev's calculations. Had these divisions not existed, Khrushchev would hardly have ventured to provoke a new crisis over Berlin. Communist psychological warfare has been not unsubtle. The anti-nuclear campaign in this country was not of their making. Indeed, at first they were opposed to it. But it is clear why they have encouraged anti-nuclear agitation in Britain ('No War over Berlin', 'Hands off Cuba'), while not permitting it at home. The Communists have no intention of losing the psychological advantage that the West's greater fear of nuclear warfare gives to them. Britain has one of the smallest Communist parties in Europe. The greater success of Communist propaganda in this country than on the Continent is at first sight curious. But the weakness of the British Communist Party is really its strength. A Communist Party on the French or Italian model would have inoculated public opinion against Soviet blandishments.

The West can be attacked frontally: in Berlin. But it can also be attacked from behind: in Africa, Asia, or Latin America. Both elements were present in Stalin's strategy. While Berlin was being blockaded, and Czechoslovakia raped, the Communists of south-east Asia were ordered on to the barricades. In 1947 a wave of violence swept India, Burma, Malaya, Indonesia, the Philippines, and Vietnam. The purpose of this strategy was twofold; to weaken the West before Marshall Aid could take effect, and to seize power in these countries during a period of political confusion. In the case of Malaya, the Communists knew that Malayan tin and rubber were vital to the West. Nevertheless, the strategy was grotesquely misconceived. Western Europe did not collapse. The liberation of India and south-east Asia was achieved under the banner of nationalism, not of communism. Instead of the favourable conditions of 1945, when they were in control of large areas of Burma, Malaya, and Vietnam, the Communists soon found themselves a hunted minority. In one country, however, the strategy was conspicuously successful: Vietnam. (Ironically, the Viet Minh had launched its offensive independently of both Stalin and Mao.) After eight years, the French suffered a severe defeat at Dien Bien Phu and threw in their hand. It was a spectacular triumph. The Viet Minh followed the guerrilla tactics Mao Tse-tung had employed against the Kuomintang. The prestige of guerrilla warfare soared. More recently, the striking success of guerrilla tactics in Cuba and their apparent triumph in Algeria and Cyprus have made guerrilla warfare seem a formidable danger. America is now engaged in a struggle with Viet Cong guerrillas in South Vietnam. The Pentagon is giving high priority to training men for guerrilla warfare. It is thought to be the form the Communist challenge is most likely to take in the next decade.

Guerrilla warfare abounds in paradoxes. It is the child of a technological age; yet its methods are as old as warfare itself. It is a kind of warfare at which intellectuals have excelled; yet it is also the most primitive and the most cruel. Its cost, to the guerrilla and the anti-guerrilla, is disproportionate. For the guerrilla, who lives off the land and steals the weapons he needs, its cost can be negligible. For the anti-guerrilla it can be ruinous. Castro showed that guerrillas can subvert and seize the apparatus of a modern state. Vietnam showed that the most sophisticated weapons are powerless against them. The Viet Minh could afford to snap their fingers at American nuclear intervention. Yet if guerrilla warfare is an alternative to thermo-nuclear warfare, it is also its complement. Both are products of that evolution towards total warfare which began when revolutionary France raised her first levies, and which Clausewitz was later to codify. Previously, wars had been fought by small professional armies and navies. The nation itself had not been mobilized. Since the French revolution, the tendency has been for the whole resources of a nation, its wealth and the morale of its population, to be drawn into the struggle.

During the nineteenth century, the drift towards total war-fare was powerfully reinforced by industrialization. In our own century, the pace has quickened alarmingly. In 1914, the distinction between combatant and non-combatant was still respected. By the thirties, the principle that an enemy's civilian population might be slaughtered by aerial bombardment was accepted by all. Guernica was merely the first practical application. The Germans had not in fact made serious preparations for this type of war. Their thinking was more conventional. It was reserved to the Anglo-Saxon powers to translate the new principle into practice in the bombing of Germany. The dropping of the first atomic bombs on Japan was no more than a logical extension of this practice. The purpose – largely unrealized in the case of Germany – was to destroy the enemy's economy and break his morale. Thermo-nuclear warfare is merely the horrific climax of this evolution.

It is the technological aspect that is usually emphasized. But that is a false emphasis. The technological breakthrough would have come in any case. More significant are the political implications of total warfare. I shall not go into all the factors assisting this evolution. But I would stress this point. The total state, as it evolved in Nazi Germany and in the Communist countries, is a product of the same factors. We know from our own experience that, in fighting a modern war, it is necessary to copy some of the characteristics of the total state: psychological warfare, conscription, economic controls, press censorship, internment of 'undesirables', direction of labour. In Britain, of course, it was a temporary and reversible process. But Germany, Russia, and China have experienced something very different. Nazism, Leninism, and Maoism have applied the principles of total war to the organization of peacetime society. The Leninist theory of a ruling élite, trained to absolute obedience within a rigid hierarchy, is essentially militarist. Of course, Lenin's party was not 'militarist' in the traditional sense. That would do small justice to Lenin's conception. If it had been, his party would not have been so successful: militarist caucuses have a poor record of political survival. Lenin's conception was more original. He conceived of politics and war, indeed of all aspects of a nation's economic, social, and intellectual life, as a unitary field of action. Unlike most socialists before him, Lenin took a serious view of war. Yet war, in his conception, was only a part of a political whole. Mao Tse-tung developed this in the light of his own experience. Guerrilla warfare was conceived, à la Clausewitz, as the continuation of the political struggle by other means. It was a logical extension of the doctrine of total war.

Two aspects of guerrilla warfare are of particular interest to us here. First, it is immune to nuclear reprisals. Secondly, it is peculiarly suited to Communist theory and practice. Many commentators consider it to be the form the Communist challenge will take in the sixties. They frequently take a pessimistic view of Western prospects. Why is this? They argue that the guerrilla is all but invulnerable. In jungle or mountain territory, the guerrilla can carry on a campaign of sabotage and terror for years, even decades. Since he has no supply lines or communications, the enemy cannot cut them. His base is invulnerable, because mobile. If he is attacked, he moves on. As a native, the guerrilla knows the terrain, the enemy does not. In general, the guerrilla lives off the land. His morale is likely to be good: those who volunteer know the risks involved. If the guerrilla is a Communist, his good morale will be stiffened by discipline and indoctrination. In Communist eyes, smallness of numbers is not a weakness but an asset. The guerrilla is a hydra. For every member he loses, he finds new recruits among the people. Wearing no uniform, he is undetectable. In Mao's famous phrase, the guerrilla 'moves among the people like a fish in water'. The guerrilla is weaker than his opponent. But he can strike where he pleases with tactical superiority. Unlike the guerrilla, his opponent has bases and communications to protect. This involves his opponent in great expense. Ruthless himself, the guerrilla is indifferent to reprisals. Indeed, since they increase the enemy's un-popularity, he welcomes them. When he is strong enough, and the enemy demoralized, the guerrilla can emerge from his jungles and mountains, and attempt a *coup d'état*. Alternatively, he can force the enemy to parley. He can demand partition of the country or a share in government. The strength of the guerrilla is that he can afford to wait. Often, his enemy cannot.

Communists have excelled at this kind of warfare. Their only serious rivals have been nationalist groups, often of the extreme Right. In the European resistance, the Communists came quickly to the fore. Their starting position was not favourable ('revolutionary defeatism', after the Nazi-Soviet pact, had alienated all patriotic groups). Yet in many cases the resistance came under their exclusive control. Yugoslavia is the most obvious example. Behind the German lines, Soviet partisans played their part in weakening the German hold on Russia. From their Yenan base, Mao's guerrillas kept up the struggle for twenty years: first against the Kuomintang of the thirties; then against the Japanese; then against the corrupt and weakened Kuomintang of the forties. In general, nationalist successes have been less spectacular. Apart from the non-Communist resistance in Europe, there have been the campaigns of Jewish terrorism in Palestine, of Grivas in Cyprus, of the F.L.N. in Algeria. Earlier, there were the campaigns of Sinn Fein in Ireland and of Lawrence against the Turks. At first sight, it looks as if terrorist and resistance movements are usually successful. In almost every case the goal of the terrorists seems to have been achieved. China and Vietnam became Communist. Russia and France were liberated. Israel and Algeria, Ireland and Cyprus became independent. This suggests that Communist adoption of the strategy might be very damaging to the West. Future guerrilla campaigns are likely to be in ex-colonial territories where the Communists can exploit nationalism against intervention by the West. By choosing the terrain carefully, the Communists can hope to nibble away at the Free World, undisturbed by Western nuclear power.

Yet the outlook is not really so pessimistic. Guerrillas have been defeated as often as they have triumphed. The effectiveness of guerrilla tactics is easily exaggerated. This is clear even from the cases I have cited. Though guerrillas played an important role in these cases, they did not play a decisive role. Europe was not liberated by her resistance movements. The Greek resistance fighters were only able to take over the country because the Germans had decided on a strategic withdrawal. Tito did not attack Belgrade until he was sure of Russian artillery and tank support. It was the Red Army that threw the Germans out of Russia, not the partisans. In China, guerrilla strategy enabled Mao to survive and retain the initiative until he was strong enough to launch a frontal attack on the Kuomintang. Yet even there the *coup de grâce* had to be delivered by Mao's conventional forces.

The one exception would appear to be Vietnam. There, surely, a guerrilla army won a decisive victory over a conventional opponent? But the Viet Minh's victory at Dien Bien Phu was not won by guerrilla tactics. Victory was won in defiance of guerrilla rules. By concentrating large forces at one point, and employing them in orthodox fashion, the Viet Minh overwhelmed the French garrison. By doing so, the Viet Minh risked encirclement. It lost the advantages of surprise, speed, and mobility. It suffered casualties twice as high as the French. The Viet Minh only won by turning itself, for the occasion, into a conventional army. The reason why the Viet Minh took this risk is plain. Dien Bien Phu was remote, almost out of range of French fighter aircraft. It was unlikely that the French could quickly relieve it. There was a political motive too. A conference on Indo-China was to be held at Geneva in the spring of 1954. The Viet Minh knew that Western opinion was divided. France was weary of the endless struggle. Britain was known to be unenthusiastic. The Americans, perhaps, were prepared to intervene. But that would have brought the counter-threat of Chinese intervention and a repetition of the Korean imbroglio. The Viet Minh judged the world political situation to be favourable to them. A crushing blow might cause the French to withdraw from Indo-China altogether. This calculation proved correct. Dien Bien Phu would not normally have been decisive: only one-sixth of the French army in Indo-China was involved. But it was politically decisive in the given circumstances, as the Viet Minh had intended it to be.

Thus the menace of guerrilla warfare is somewhat reduced in scale. On the one hand, it is seen to be merely auxiliary to conventional warfare, a useful but not indispensable diversion. The Nazis would have been defeated had there been no resistance movement in Europe at all. In China, certainly, it was something more. But China is very large, and her political confusion at the time was abnormal, and unlikely to recur elsewhere. (Mao insisted that the *size* of China was a major factor in his success: Congo, India, and Brazil are perhaps the only countries where a similar strategy could succeed.) On the other hand, guerrilla warfare is only successful where the general political situation is favourable. This was the case in Palestine. Later experience, in Malaya, Kenya, and Cyprus, suggests that Jewish terrorism could have been crushed. But external political pressure on Britain to leave Palestine was very strong. The United Nations had voted for the creation of a Jewish State. The idea had the support of Russia and America and a large part of world opinion. In 1947-8, Britain was rapidly withdrawing from her commitments as an imperial power. It was political pressure that forced Britain out of Palestine, not the activities of the terrorists.

A closer look at events in Vietnam, Cyprus, and Algeria confirms that guerrillas are only successful when the external political situation is favourable. This situation, of course, is a major factor in their own calculations. Thus, contrary to what is often thought, the fanatic seldom makes a successful guerrilla. The successful guerrilla must be ready for political compromise. In Cyprus, Eoka appeared to have 'won'. But the original aim of the war – Enosis – was not realized. In fact, Eoka had not even 'won' in a military sense: it had been fought to a stalemate. Sensibly, Eoka accepted the only compromise possible in a complex political situation. But this was a good deal less than Enosis. Similarly, the Viet Minh accepted a solution apparently less favourable than they might have expected. They agreed to the partition of Vietnam, and made no claim to Laos or Cambodia. This was shrewd politics. They knew that Dien Bien Phu had not brought a decision. By demanding their full pound of flesh, they would have ensured continuance of the war, and perhaps American intervention. By compromising, they ensured French withdrawal from Indo-China. They calculated that the rest of Indo-China would fall to them eventually. Their hopes were not fulfilled in the short run. But America is now fighting a hard guerrilla war to save South Vietnam from the Communists. She has already renounced the attempt to protect Laos from similar infiltration. From the West's point of view, Laos has been written off. If South Vietnam is not defended, the whole of Indo-China will be in Communist hands. Siam, Burma, and Malaya will be directly threatened. India's flank will have been turned.

But the prospects for the guerrilla are less bright than is usually thought. Astonishingly, there seems to be only one case in which a guerrilla campaign has been successful without assistance from abroad, and without a final switch from guerrilla to conventional tactics: Cuba. But in Cuba the resistance of authority appears to have been very half-hearted, and sympathy with the guerrillas general. Castro's take-over approximated to the traditional Latin American *coup d'état* – down to the ex-dictator boarding a plane and taking his bank-balance with him. This situation could well recur, particularly in Latin America. But, on present evidence, Castro's success is atypical. Against the usually cited cases of guerrilla success – Yugoslavia, Vietnam, Algeria – must be set the less publicized cases of total failure. Most of the actions initiated during Stalin's offensive are in this category: Greece, Malaya, Burma, India, Indonesia, the Philippines. There is also the case of the Mau Mau rising in Kenya. In all these cases, guerrillas were defeated, though not without great hardship and expense. How was it done? The answer is of some interest. For it bears not only on the question of the best tactics for the West in dealing with this particular threat, but on the West's general strategy in the Cold War.

There was no one method. But the variety of methods is itself an indication of what the modern guerrilla must contend with. Few anti-guerrilla campaigns have been won by military action alone. But there is one case where a conventional military blow was decisive: Greece. Here, as elsewhere, victory was won by a reversal of the guerrilla's own strategy. Traditionally, the guerrilla's strength is that he is invulnerable; he has no base to defend. The moment he offends against his own precept, he becomes vulnerable. General Markos' Greek Communist guerrillas did precisely that. They were dependent on a base at Vitsos, near the Greek–Albanian border, across which arms and supplies were smuggled. In the summer of 1949, after three years of inconclusive fighting (though the balance was tilting towards the government forces), the regular Greek army put an end to the war in little more than a week by a direct strike at this base. Other factors were at work: the closure of the Yugoslav border, the setting up of a national defence corps, lavish American economic and military aid. But this one blow was decisive. The switch to conventional warfare, as at Dien Bien Phu, is the necessary preliminary to the last phase of a guerrilla campaign. But it is also the moment of greatest danger. By abandoning his familiar tactics, the guerrilla makes possible his destruction by conventional methods.

But conventional methods alone are seldom effective. This was recognized by the French officers who had fought in Indo-China, and were taken prisoner by the Viet Minh after Dien Bien Phu. These officers were determined to apply what they had learned about Communist tactics to the struggle against the nationalist F.L.N. However wrong-headed, the conclusions they drew are of considerable interest. Thus General Chassin wrote in October 1954:

> It is time for the army to cease being the *grande muette*. The time has come for the free world, unless it wishes to die a violent death, to apply certain of its adversaries' methods. One of these methods, probably the most important, resides in the ideological role which, behind the Iron Curtain, has been assigned to the military forces.

In a similar vein, Colonel Lacheroy:

> One will never insist enough on this point: propaganda directed from the base of *mild-mannered democracy* will never be effective, while on the contrary it will achieve maximum efficiency from the base of a *clean, hard organization of parallel hierarchies*. [My italics.]

The intellectual implications of this need not be stressed. They were spelt out after the Algiers coup of 13 May 1958 by another of the 'Algiers colonels', Colonel Trinquier:

> Call me a Fascist if you like; but we must make the people easy to manage; everybody's acts must be controlled.

Fortunately, the Algiers colonels were not given the opportunity to put their brave new theories into practice. General de Gaulle proved to be a liberal autocrat. But what had happened is of great interest: in fighting against a totalitarian opponent, the colonels had adopted his methods. That the free world cannot be defended by methods which contradict its own assumptions did not occur to them. Yet the conclusions they drew from their defeat in Indo-China were not wholly wrong. France's reliance on conventional methods had indeed been her undoing. The Viet Minh owed its victory in large part to its intelligence network, its disciplined hierarchy, its propaganda apparatus. The Algiers colonels were not wrong in thinking that France would lose Algeria if she did not learn to fight the F.L.N. on the political and psychological plane. Belatedly, these methods were tried out in Algeria. Yet France lost Algeria as she lost Indo-China. Why?

The answer is as encouraging to the democratic anti-Communist as it is flattering to an Englishman. For France's failure in Algeria and Indo-China, and Britain's relative success in Malaya, Cyprus, and Kenya, are related to a difference in political mentality. Earlier, I argued that the Continent understood the Fascist and Communist mentality better than we in Britain. I argued, further, that a failure of understanding lay behind British readiness to conciliate Hitler and Khrushchev. I believe this to be true. Yet British success at this barbarous, and highly ideological, kind of warfare suggests the opposite. Colonel Blimp seems to have mastered the challenge better than the Algiers colonels. Of course, the comparison is not quite fair: Vietnam and Algeria were bigger problems than anything the British had to face. But the thing cannot be seen in isolation. If Algerian and Vietnamese nationalism were more serious problems, that was the result of French colonial policy. By her policies, France had alienated her friends. By hers, Britain had made new friends. In both cases, policies were rooted in different political mentalities.

Colonel Blimp and his political advisers, who had not read a page of Mao Tse-tung, had the advantage in two respects: they were more empirical, and they understood the political nature of the struggle. Empiricism was an important factor. Despite their experience with the European resistance during the war, the British found that at the end of two years of fighting in Malaya they had made little progress. The main fault was that of the French in Indo-China: reliance on conventional tactics. It was soon realized that guerrillas must be fought by guerrilla methods. Instead of large-scale jungle sweeps, small parties of local troops under British officers were sent into the jungle to live as guerrillas. Meanwhile, the Chinese squatters who supplied the terrorists with food were resettled. In Kenya, the technique of penetration was further refined. Not only the jungle, but the mind of the terrorist himself must be penetrated. This was done by forming 'converted' Mau Mau terrorists into counter-gangs. These gangs penetrated the Mau Mau network in the forests, gathered information, undermined morale, joined up with genuine Mau Mau gangs and took them prisoner. Other methods were developed, often of remarkable unconventionality. In Malaya and in Kenya, the confessions of surrendered terrorists were broadcast by air over jungle hide-outs. In Cyprus it was the helicopter, able to move faster than Eoka intelligence, that was the decisive weapon.

Yet none of these methods was decisive. What finally destroyed guerrilla strength was the reversal of Mao Tse-tung's presupposition: the guerrillas could no longer 'move among the people like a fish in water'. The methods by which the guerrillas were isolated were entirely traditional. In Malaya, since the terrorists were almost exclusively Chinese, Malayan nationalism could be exploited against them. By protecting Chinese residents from reprisals, the anti-Communists among them could be mobilized. By a liberal colonial policy – with a prospect of complete independence – the political appeal of the guerrillas could be offset. (It was French stubbornness, and the deep mistrust French policy had awakened, that prevented France from pursuing the same policy in Indo-China and Algeria.) A generous amnesty was offered to individual terrorists, and this quickly undermined guerrilla morale. Indeed, the lesson of Malaya is that leniency, not counter-terror, is the effective weapon.

How far is this typical? It is often assumed that victory goes to the more ruthless opponent. This is clearly true of the contest between Mihailovitch and Tito for control of the Yugoslav resistance movement. Mihailovitch's reluctance to expose the population to reprisals caused him to withdraw from the struggle, and finally to collaborate with the Germans against Tito. Tito saw that savage German reprisals only played into his hands. His greater ruthlessness became a political asset. But that this is not invariably true is apparent from the Germans' own experience. The Nazis were prepared to use the most ruthless methods, and did so in the early years of the war. But the most ruthless methods were not found to be the most effective. By the end of the war, instructions were being issued to anti-guerrilla forces not to take arbitrary reprisals. Guerrillas were to be persuaded to surrender by offers of lenient treatment. The Germans had understood Mao's dictum that a guerrilla war is a war for the allegiance of the people. Prepared to be ruthless, they learnt from experience that leniency pays better. That the same is true for the guerrilla is shown by the sudden switch in tactics made by the Malayan Communists in 1951. The former policy of indiscriminate murder and sabotage was dropped. It was realized that the Party was antagonizing the very people on whose support it must depend. This change of front was a clear sign that the terrorists had been forced on to the defensive. To the people of Malaya it seemed – as indeed it was – an indication of impending defeat. By 1951, the Communists had lost the initiative and were not to recover it.

Thus the West has no reason for pessimism. The Cuban situation may recur. But against the techniques of subversion from within there can be no real defence. When Castro first rode into Havana, he was not a Communist. Once the Communist Party had become indispensable to his regime, through the destruction of all competitors, Castro became its prisoner. It seems doubtful whether a more conciliatory American policy could have prevented this development. (When Castro was negotiating for America to buy the Cuban sugar crop in May 1959, it appears to have been his side that sabotaged the negotiations, not the Americans.) But this had little to do with guerrilla warfare, which the Cuban Communists long opposed. It is comparable rather to the 1948 Communist take-over in Czechoslovakia. In the field of guerrilla warfare, the techniques available to the modern anti-guerrilla are formidable. If rigorously applied, and accompanied by political and social reform, they are likely to be successful.

I have said guerrilla warfare is essentially political warfare.

But the Communists have shown no such striking aptitude at it as is often assumed. Nor is this surprising. The Leninist technique is a technique for the seizure of power by a minority. The failures of communism in Greece and Malaya demonstrate the Communists' inability to win the allegiance of a people in open political combat. The policies Britain pursued in Malaya and Kenya were not different in kind from the policies she pursued in her other colonies. She won the allegiance of the people by giving economic, medical, and technical aid, by supporting the libertarian, socially progressive forces against the forces of totalitarianism and feudalism, and by offering a prospect of political independence. It is these policies the Communists fear most. For they offer an alternative to communism that is both more efficient and more attractive. The Fascist theories of the Algiers colonels were a counsel of despair. They were also ineffective. The techniques of 'mild-mannered democracy,' can be shown to have worked.

V. A Prospect for John Bull

CHAPTER 14

EUROPE AND THE BOMB

BRITAIN is said to lack national purpose. But national purpose is a paradoxical thing. Nations that have it do not speak of it; nations that speak of it do not have it. That was Britain's case for the greater part of her history. If we speak of it now, the inference is plain: we speak of what we do not have. But the root of our embarrassment goes deeper. It is not to make a mystique of nationhood to say that it cannot be reduced to a formula. That is a matter of observation. A nation that becomes conscious of a lack of purpose is easily enslaved to a formula. That was Germany's case after Versailles. Formulas impoverish and constrict; but constriction may come to be preferred to confusion. Yet what is the politician to do? What is conscious cannot be made unconscious; the public cries out for a formula. We have seen this at work in Britain in recent years: the Three Interlocking Circles; the Special Relationship; Going into Europe; the Summit; Interdependence. It is a melancholy procession. Each formula contained a measure of truth. Yet each was offered as a shortcut, a charm, a gimmick.

I have included 'Going into Europe' among the gimmicks. Let me add that I do so as a last-ditch European. Though a socialist, I believe Mr Macmillan's application to join the Common Market to have been the most courageous decision made by a British government since 1945. What I criticize is not the policy, but the presentation of it. The political significance of going into Europe was never explained, the difficulties never publicly examined. The policy was presented as a gimmick. The irony of this is now plain.

What Mr Macmillan failed to do in eighteen months, General de Gaulle achieved at a single press conference. With French logic, he explained to the British why they have no alternative but to go into Europe. The immediate re-action has been a certain revulsion from Europe. But I believe that a new Europeanism has been created in Britain – and also in Europe – by de Gaulle's rejection of us. It is still inchoate; but, once articulated, I believe it will destroy Gaullism itself. Meanwhile, if de Gaulle has destroyed the gimmick, that is all to the good. The real arguments for going into Europe can now be spelt out. Can Europe provide Britain with a national purpose? Put in this form, the ques-tion invites the answer no. The anti-Europeans were quick to point out the fallacy. It may be that European countries have a more vital sense of national purpose. But a national purpose is not a *deus ex machina*. About this the anti-Euro-peans were quite right. The anti-Europeans, however, encouraged equal and opposite fallacies in their own ranks. Britain's national purpose was to be provided by the Com-monwealth, or by the nations of the underdeveloped world. In both cases, the fallacy was the same. An external agency was invoked to provide Britain with a national purpose.

I believe there were better arguments for going in. They were not always those actually given. Indeed, I believe the issue was frequently misunderstood. Thus, a symposium published by the magazine *Encounter* showed that of 110 British intellectuals asked for an opinion 77 were in favour of going into Europe and only 17 opposed (16 were unde-cided). It seems a conclusive majority. But one feature of the symposium was striking: few British intellectuals seemed to regard going into Europe as a *political* problem. Many contributors said that they felt unable to judge the economic issues involved; but few doubted the primacy of economics. The correctness of the government's presentation of the case was accepted without question. In the absence of politics, cultural arguments came into the fore. Arguments for or against going into Europe were based on cultural predilections: Insularity versus Cosmopolitanism: Empiricism versus Metaphysics. The consensus of opinion was that British culture had become provincial; a gust of fresh air would do it no harm. That may be so. But what is its relevance to Britain's joining the Common Market? That British culture is provincial is probably true. But Europe can no more provide Britain with a healthy cosmopolitan outlook (if that is what is called for) than it can provide Britain with a national purpose. Such arguments have a suspiciously mechanical ring. Does a historical correlation exist between the intensity of British involvement with European culture and Britain's political alignment? Plainly not. Britain was at war with Catholic France and allied with Protestant Germany for a great part of her history. Yet which has influenced Britain the more? That post-war England extended a cool welcome to Heidegger and Sartre may be evidence of provinciality. But we ought not to blame this on the customs officials at Dover and Boulogne.

Better arguments for entering were provided by the anti-Europeans. The reasons given by the anti-Europeans for staying out were often reasons for going in. Far Right and far Left were agreed that the Common Market was a 'Cold War grouping'. Whereas the Commonwealth, with its neutralist majority, provided a bridge between races and creeds, the Common Market was a White Man's Club. That the European neutrals were to be excluded showed that the Common Market was dedicated to 'Cold War aims'. The argument is worth examining. It shows, I believe, that the anti-Europeans had a better understanding of the Common Market on this point than many pro-Europeans. Lord Sandwich, in a letter to the *Observer*, commenting on a pro-Market article by Sir William Hayter, had this to say:

Sir William, secure in Cold War theories of the 1950s, appears to think that the result of Britain's approach to the Common Market and subsequent withdrawal will be to institute centripetal tendencies in the E.E.C. itself, and that the sole gainer will be Mr Khrushchev. . . . But would an easement in the Cold War,

Britain's primary objective, be obtained by this [going into Europe]? Does our joining the Common Market help Lord Home's policy in Central Europe? Mr Khrushchev seems to think not, and he is a party to the peaceful settlement of the German problem. By joining the Common Market Britain helps to perpetuate the Cold War.

It so happens that my sympathies are with Sir William. But I would make this point: though the views of Sir William Hayter and Lord Sandwich are diametrically opposed, both discuss the Common Market in terms of power politics. They treat the economic and cultural arguments as secondary.

Britain's going into Europe will bring about a re-orientation of political and military power in Europe and the world. Necessarily, this reorientation will take place in the context of the Cold War. Britain's entry or non-entry is therefore an important factor in the Cold War. I do not believe, with Lord Sandwich, that the Common Market 'perpetuates the Cold War'. Western Europe did not start the Cold War, nor can she have an interest in perpetuating it. The origins of the Cold War in Europe were Russia's vast military preponderance and her militant anti-Western ideology. It is possible, though not I think plausible, to argue that the ideological hostility has 'withered away'. But it is not possible to argue that Western Europe has ever presented a threat to the Soviet Union. Stalin's offensive was launched when Europe was weaker than at any time in her history. Indeed, that is why the Kremlin launched it. Western Europe has now recovered much of her strength. But she is still weak in relation to Russia. Nato can still only muster 23 divisions on the Central European front, against the Warsaw Pact's 40–60 divisions. According to Liddell Hart, even in nuclear war attack requires a 3–1 superiority over defence. These figures show one thing beyond doubt. The Russians may lack the will to attack, but they do not lack the means. The West, even if it had the will, lacks the means.

To assert that the Europe of the Six is a 'Cold War

grouping' is, in one sense, to assert the obvious. Europe's urge to unity was born out of a sense of overwhelming Russian power. I said earlier that though an understanding of the Cold War cannot provide Britain with a national purpose, it can provide the context in which a decision must be made. The Cold War cannot provide the West with a sense of purpose, because the West's role in it is essentially passive. It is in the nature of the conflict that the West must adopt the strategic defensive, and the Communists the strategic offensive. But the strategic defensive is often psychologically demoralizing; it encourages the 'Maginot mentality'. Nevertheless, the democratic West has no alternative. (The alternative offered by the Algiers colonels was self-contradictory; the West they planned for would no longer have been democratic.) Yet the story of Europe's recovery suggests that this is not wholly true. The Cold War did not provide her with a national purpose; but neither did it demoralize her. Yet Europe's exposure to the Cold War was more searing than anything post-war Britain experienced. Evidently, it is not quite true that the Cold War provided Europe with no more than a context. It seems also to have acted as a stimulus.

Nor am I thinking only in terms of the military threat. The military power of Western Europe has been painfully rebuilt. This has helped Europe to recover her self-confidence. But the most spectacular evidence of European revival has not been in the field of political unity or military coordination. It has been in fields less directly associated with the Cold War challenge – particularly in economics. It is the economic recovery of Europe that has given her people a new sense of national purpose. The forty years of European economic stagnation have been overcome. The 4–8 per cent growth-rates Europe has enjoyed during the fifties will slow down. But they are still likely to exceed the 2–3 per cent growth-rates Britain and America have become accustomed to. Yet only indirectly is this recovery a response to the Cold War. To Marxist–Leninists it is a challenge, in that it has falsified Marx's predictions about the future of capitalism. But the recovery of capitalism is not due to the Cold War. It is the product of other factors: Keynesian fiscal techniques, scientific and technological advance, the countervailing power of workers' organizations. The recovery might easily have come about had Russian communism never existed. The Marshall Plan certainly took shape in a Cold War context. Quite apart from the Cold War, however, a weak, depressed Europe was not in America's interest. The Cold War acted as a stimulus to European recovery. But, once under way, that recovery became a force in its own right. Western Europe did not after all develop a 'Maginot mentality'. Stalin's offensive was the indirect and unwitting agent of her recovery of national purpose.

The critics of the Common Market as a 'Cold War grouping' do not have this in mind. They are worried by its political and military implications. During the Berlin crisis, these critics accused General de Gaulle and Dr Adenauer of inflexibility. This was contrasted with Britain's undogmatic approach. 'Jaw-jaw is better than war-war,' it was said: to refuse to negotiate was therefore tantamount to warmongering. Both views had their logic. If Khrushchev wanted the settlement of the German question, it was sensible to negotiate. If Khrushchev wanted the unsettlement of the German question, it was not. If concessions would cool Mr Khrushchev's ardour, it was right to conciliate him. If the opposite were true, conciliation might make him more aggressive. The doves would then be the warmongers; and the hawks the bringers of peace. This division of opinion was one between peoples as well as between governments. When Dr Adenauer told British journalists that 'an urge to join Europe is incompatible with appeasement of Russia', he expressed the view of his countrymen. That de Gaulle believed the Anglo-Saxons were again ready, as at Yalta, to sell out European interests may be taken for granted.

Perhaps the British approach was the correct one. But it was clearly unfortunate that Europe had come to think of

Britain in this way. Britain's application to join the Common Market had been made in July 1961: two months after Khrushchev's Vienna ultimatum, three weeks before the Berlin Wall. Far from showing solidarity with European interests, the British public's coolness towards the fate of the Berliners and East Germans was quickly demonstrated. Lord Home's anti-Soviet speeches were popular on the Continent. At home he was accused of warmongering. Britain's 'soft' posture was arousing new suspicions just when Continental good will had become vital to her. No political groups were better disposed to Britain's application than the German Social-Democrats and Free Democrats. Yet this British posture was calculated to offend their susceptibilities. Of course, Britain's stance may have been right and her application to join the Market wrong. That is what most anti-Europeans thought. In this they were consistent. The inflexibility of Dr Adenauer and General de Gaulle confirmed their suspicions that the Common Market was a 'Cold War grouping'.

The logic of this was not lost on General de Gaulle. Ironically, however, it was not for appeasement of Russia that the General slammed the door on Britain, but for appeasement of America. The motives for the General's action have been much debated. A connexion with the Nassau agreement has been officially denied. Nevertheless, I believe General de Gaulle's reading of this agreement to have been the decisive factor. What was that reading? General de Gaulle evidently interpreted the Nassau agreement, not only as Britain's abdication of nuclear status, but as Britain's abdication as a European power. In the General's mind, the two abdications are intimately connected. The connexion lies in de Gaulle's equation of political sovereignty with control over nuclear weapons. He argues that Western Europe is potentially as strong, in terms of manpower and economic strength, as Russia or America. It is anachronistic that Western Europe should be as much the satellite of America as Poland and Hungary are satellites of the Soviet

Union. Yet Suez showed the one as clearly as Hungary showed the other. Western Europe's freedom of action is limited by an American as well as a Soviet veto. (Whether the Suez adventure was politically justifiable is a different matter.)

Yet the strength of Western Europe exists only in potentiality. It can become a reality only if Europe acquires a political framework. It is that which has been lacking in Europe's remarkable recovery. The Common Market is not – as the British anti-Europeans pointed out – a genuine political organization; it is a bureaucracy. With this European federalists would agree. But General de Gaulle is known to have little use for European federalism. Why is this? The reason is said to be de Gaulle's irrational nationalism. He cannot bear that France should be submerged in a *machin*, a faceless, supranational authority. I do not agree. De Gaulle's objection to supranational institutions is entirely rational. It is bound up with his conception of nuclear sovereignty. De Gaulle argues that authority over the ultimate weapons cannot be delegated to a committee. There is nothing unorthodox or irrational about this. It is the view taken by the Kennedy administration. Indeed, reduced to its simplest terms, de Gaulle's proposal is that de Gaulle should be Europe's Kennedy. The proposal may be unacceptable. But the assumptions underlying it are rational enough. Thinking as he does, de Gaulle could not but reject Britain's application to join his Europe.

Can we fault this French logic? Let us leave aside for a moment the technical considerations. His critics claim that these will render the *force de frappe* obsolete before it has come into service. But French military thinkers (and General de Gaulle is one of the most distinguished military thinkers of his generation) are evidently persuaded that the *force de frappe* will be a credible deterrent. For the sake of argument, let us grant this. On what other grounds can the argument be faulted? I believe it is a great deal less easy to do so than many commentators assume. I have already

pointed to the irony of the present contest between Britain
and France: France stands today where Britain stood fifteen
years ago. Then, it was we who reckoned with an American
withdrawal and decided to build our own nuclear arsenal.
True, the technical difficulties were not understood as they
are today. But the decision to build an independent deterrent was a *political* decision. And its motives were no different
from those that now impel General de Gaulle. It may be
said that whereas Britain's main thought was to keep
America in Europe, General de Gaulle is determined to get
her out. But that is not quite true. General de Gaulle does
not like the Americans any more than he likes us. But it is
not a question of sentiment. De Gaulle believes that the
American presence in Europe is an anomaly, the temporary
product of Europe's weakness since 1945. By the end of the
sixties, Europe will be strong enough to look to her own
defence. Her population is equal to that of Russia and her
satellites. Her industrial power is comparable.

.The truth of this, in simple facts and figures, is indisput-
able. But, in de Gaulle's view, there is one thing lacking:
nuclear sovereignty. Thus, de Gaulle's views would be
what they are even if he held America in high esteem and
affection. (We should remember that de Gaulle did not hide
his admiration for President Kennedy's actions during Cuba
Week.) It is merely that he regards America's withdrawal in
the long run as inevitable. But this is no different from
Britain's attitude in 1947. No doubt, Britain did hold America in high esteem and affection. But this did not prevent us
from distrusting America's isolationist instincts. Indeed, the
British independent deterrent was doubly the child of mistrust. In the first place, America had refused to share her
atomic secrets with her wartime ally. But Britain was un-
willing to entrust her defence to America in perpetuity. It is
often said that, since the British deterrent represents no more
than two per cent of the West's nuclear arsenal, Britain is
foolish to 'duplicate' the American effort. But that is to miss
the point. The decision to build the deterrent was a *political*

decision. It had a built-in anti-American component from the start. If Britain's trust in America were perfect, why should she embark on an independent deterrent at all? This mistrust had nothing to do with sentiment. It was a political mistrust. As such, it was in no way different from General de Gaulle's present attitude. The difference is that Britain and France have exchanged roles.

It is said that in 1945 Britain could have had the political leadership of Europe for the asking. I believe this to be true. I believe that to have refused it was a blunder for which we shall pay for decades to come. Certainly, Britain could not have done for Europe what America did through the Marshall Plan. American economic, technical, and military help would have been required. But America was never in a position to give Europe political leadership. Britain, in her post-war confidence and prestige, was. In fact, America never aspired to organize Europe politically. She encouraged efforts at European unification from afar. But she did not try to make of Nato more than a military alliance on conventional lines. It was not until the accession of President Kennedy that America formally asserted her primacy in the alliance. Ironically, it was then too late. But, in 1945, Britain could certainly have done for Europe what General de Gaulle aspires to do for her now. If she had taken the lead, the hesitations of the past few years might never have occurred. However, that is all spilt milk. It is no longer a question of whether Britain should lead. It seems that we shall be lucky to be admitted at all. How are the mighty fallen! It seems, likewise, that we are ready to put in America the confidence we refused to put in her fifteen years ago. Why should this be? What has changed to make acceptable now what was not acceptable then? Many commentators would return a technological answer. What was technically possible for a middle-sized country fifteen years ago is beyond her capability today.

Once again, let us leave technological considerations aside. The crucial question is this: has Europe's development during the fifties made American political leadership more acceptable than it was fifteen years ago? Plainly not. In the first years after 1947, Europe had little choice but to accept American leadership. The contrast between the vast war-time increase in the power and wealth of America, and Europe's relative post-war enfeeblement, was overwhelming. Britain's prestige and self-confidence were still high, but she was loath to share her good fortune with others. The situation is now very different. Europe has fully recovered her economic self-confidence. It is America that faces balance of payments problems and must try to stimulate a flagging economy. The Common Market is a centre of world economic influence second only to the United States. The Common Market is less self-sufficient economically than America. But, paradoxically, this increases her political leverage in the world. A permanent buyer's market in commodities means that the world must come to her door. She is also a major source of capital for the underdeveloped nations. Her potential political leverage is therefore very great. In the military field, the main weight of European defence rests on the German Bundeswehr, which now outnumbers the Anglo-Saxon contingents. If American troops withdrew from Europe tomorrow, the nuclear crisis would become acute. But there is no doubt that the European members of Nato could find the men to replace these troops if they were so minded. The factor that ensures Europe's continuing dependence on America is her nuclear backwardness. It is this that de Gaulle intends to correct.

Plainly, American leadership is inherently less acceptable to Europe than it was fifteen years ago. Again, it is not a question of sentiment. It is simply that Europe has outgrown American tutelage. Yet the tendency of the Kennedy administration has been to assert American political leadership within the alliance. Nor is there any doubt of what President Kennedy bases this claim on: America's near-monopoly of Western nuclear power. Thus, while the standpoints of the French and American presidents are opposed, they subscribe to the same logic. They believe that nuclear power is the *sine qua non* of world-political leadership. They argue that the control over nuclear power cannot be delegated. The tendency of any country is to keep its most powerful weapons in its own hands. In the nuclear field technical considerations seem to reinforce this aim. Indeed, they seem to exclude any other solution. This is as apparent to President de Gaulle as to President Kennedy; their logic is identical. There are other considerations. De Gaulle does not deny the advantages of a reassertion of strong political leadership within the Western alliance. His support of President Kennedy during Cuba Week shows that he welcomes it. Nevertheless, he argues that the reassertion of American authority at this juncture is anachronistic. President Kennedy has put forward his claim to paramountcy at a time when American power is stagnating and that of Europe rising. De Gaulle agrees with Kennedy that the Western alliance suffered from the passivity of the Eisenhower era. But in attempting to reassert America's leadership he is running counter to the facts of rising European power. Kennedy is involved here, he believes, in a fundamental contradiction. It is no coincidence that Washington's relations with Paris and Bonn have been worse during the first three years of the Kennedy era than at any time during the past fifteen years.

It is easy to sympathize with Washington. Her European allies are an unruly lot. Moscow, in the eastern half of Europe, has a simpler task. But this is only partly because Moscow deals with satellites and Washington with free nations. Washington too has ways of bringing pressure to bear; and Khrushchev cannot ride roughshod over his satellites' feelings as Stalin could. The difference is inherent in the internal power-structure of the alliances. Consider the following figures: Russia has a population of 200 million; her satellites a population of 100 million. That is a proportion of two-to-one in her favour. America has a population of 180 million; her satellites a population of 180 million (if we take the Common Market alone) or 330 million (if we take Nato, Spain, and the European neutrals). That is very nearly a proportion of two-to-one against. In military and economic terms, the preponderance of Russia over Eastern Europe is greater even than the preponderance of the United States over Western Europe fifteen years ago. Further, Eastern Europe is made up of many small states. Even the largest of these – Poland – has no more than fifteen per cent of the population of the Soviet Union. Western Europe, on the other hand, is dominated by four large countries. The average population of each of these countries is thirty per cent of that of the United States. This structure is a factor militating against the domination of Western Europe by any one of the four powers. But it is also a factor militating against the domination of Western Europe by America. We may detest the regimes Russia has imposed on Eastern Europe. But we cannot deny that Russian domination is implicit in the facts of power. Russia's satellites are small, weak, and divided among themselves. Yet, even if they were not, no combination of forces could hope to challenge the supremacy of Soviet power. But this is not the situation in Western Europe. Any of the three larger powers, with or without the minor ones, could hope to challenge United States supremacy with some success. That challenge is already implicit in the Common Market. It follows that a combination of all the European powers – though its diversity would be a weakening factor – would be a very formidable grouping. This Europe would be potentially stronger than either North America or the powers of the Warsaw Pact.

The accent, of course, must fall on 'potentially'. Without a political framework, without a clear pattern of authority, this potential cannot be realized. Yet the structure of Western Europe, which permits it to challenge America, reduces its chances of developing a pattern of authority from within itself. That the four main states are of equal size and power makes it difficult for one state to dominate the rest. But a combination of two large states will antagonize not only the other two but the smaller states into the bargain. This would clearly be the effect of a narrow Franco-German *entente*. The European federalist would argue that the only solution is a genuinely supranational authority: a responsible European parliament, perhaps, elected by universal suffrage. It is an attractive notion. But I believe General de Gaulle is right in thinking that it could not work. Certain economic powers can be delegated to a supranational authority like the Common Market Commission or the Coal and Steel Community. But I do not think it is realistic to expect nations to surrender responsibility for their most vital concerns, particularly where the security of the nation is at stake. I believe General de Gaulle's objections to this kind of Europe are realistic. The system could not be made to work. Nor, I think, would many people in this country disagree with his judgement. Unfortunately, the solution General de Gaulle proposes is no more realistic. He offers himself as Europe's Kennedy. That this is unworkable is implicit in the figures I have given. That Europe should voluntarily accept de Gaulle as her leader, entrusting her nuclear sovereignty to him (though, no doubt, contributing to the cost of his nuclear arsenal), would be a rational solution. But it would not be a realistic one. For if the larger European states are restless under the leadership of a power three times their size, how should they accept the leadership of a power equal, or, in the case of West Germany, inferior to themselves? The political balance would be impossible to maintain. The new alliance would be more unstable than the old.

What is the solution? I fear my analysis has been largely negative. But the problems of political control over nuclear weapons are too easily glossed over. It is said that the British Polaris deterrent will be both 'integrated with the U.S. deterrent' and 'available for independent action in moments of supreme national emergency'. I believe those critics are right who argue that if the deterrent is not truly independent it is not worth having at all. There is indeed no reason for 'duplicating' the American effort. The independence of the deterrent is its *only* justification. Whether this will be the case with Polaris is not clear. But does Britain need a deterrent? It is widely accepted that we do not. But to those who say this, the question should perhaps be put in reverse: are you prepared for Britain to surrender her share in the development of these techniques *in perpetuity*? Are you prepared to accept the division of the world into a Soviet and American (and perhaps a French and Chinese) sphere of influence *in perpetuity*? If Britain pulls out of the nuclear race at this stage, it is extremely unlikely that she will be able to return. The next decade may bring a technical breakthrough, enabling the smaller powers to make their deterrents credible. It is true that the expense is great, and constantly growing. But the pace of technical development has been so rapid in the past decade, and Britain is relatively so well placed in the competition, that it would seem unwise to throw in our hand now. It is not so certain that at some future stage brains will not count more, and money less, than they do at present.

I do not think it can be denied that there are cases in which the possession of an independent deterrent might count. Without it, we should be exposed to nuclear blackmail. It would mean that we could not undertake any action, in any part of the world, that did not have the approval of the United States. Those who reject the deterrent are assenting to this limitation. They are conceding that Britain must bow to the wishes of one or both of the great powers in case of disagreement. Perhaps that is inevitable. But those who reject the independent deterrent ought to be frank about the implications. It is certainly not compatible with anti-Americanism. Again, Britain would lose far more of her sovereignty by this step than she ever would by going into Europe. Are these limitations acceptable? The counter-arguments, based on an opposition to the spread of nuclear weapons, are not compelling. Unilateralists argue that Britain's abandonment of nuclear weapons would encourage others to do likewise. But is this so? Most non-nuclear powers are non-nuclear by necessity, not by conviction. It has yet to be shown that any nation that is in a position to make or obtain them has explicitly renounced them. It is certain that France and China, and probably other powers, will proceed with the development of nuclear weapons, regardless of Britain's actions. Britain's renunciation might be noble, but it would find few imitators.

I believe, then, that Britain should carry on with her independent deterrent. I believe, further, that Britain possesses in her present nuclear expertise the bargaining power with which she could come to terms with Gaullism. What we are able to offer the Italians and the Germans in the way of nuclear know-how is superior to anything the French can offer for many years to come. Equally, what we have to offer the French would save them great expense of trouble, time, and treasure. The bargaining power possessed by the United States is proportionately much greater. On taking office in 1958, General de Gaulle proposed a threefold directorium for Nato: America, Britain, and France. Britain and the United States ignored the proposal. Yet it could still be revived. De Gaulle, to put it crudely, could still be bought. Alternatively, it might be necessary to by-pass the French, and open the directorium to the Germans and the Italians. This would be far from ideal, but it would be better than the nightmare of 'fifteen-fingers-on-the-trigger'. We should have to weigh the advisability of giving the West Germans control over nuclear weapons. I believe that this would be less 'dangerous' than is usually supposed. Earlier, I gave reasons for thinking that it worries Khrushchev less than it worries commentators in the West. Experience does not suggest that nations controlling these weapons become more reckless. On the contrary, their possession seems to have a distinctly sobering effect. I believe this applies to Germany, France, China, and ourselves as much as to Russia and America.

The bargaining power that we and the Americans possess

is considerable. Indeed, the smaller the chances of making the French deterrent credible, the stronger our bargaining power. It could be used to force General de Gaulle to abandon his bid for supremacy and permit Britain to join in shaping the future of Europe. It is clear that the Five would welcome such a development. With Dr Adenauer's retirement, it does not seem likely that Germany will continue to support France against America. A directorium has the advantage over a supranational authority that its members are directly responsible to a democratically elected government. But there must be no veto. If they cannot agree, each must be free to take independent action. By working out possible responses to Soviet initiatives beforehand, contingency planning should be able to assist political coordination. It is the Russians who must be kept guessing, not the Nato governments. Even alone, there is a great deal that Britain can do. But we are likely to be able to count on the support of the Americans, if they are willing to abandon their own 'Gaullist' claims to paramountcy. A close reading of de Gaulle's career does not suggest that he is inflexible when confronted with overwhelming strength. The alternative is plain: General de Gaulle has indicated that he expects Britain, outside Europe, to suffer a rapid decline in power and prestige. When the process is complete, we shall be ready to accept his terms. Meanwhile, France and America will enter a phase of increasingly bitter struggle. The contest will end, either in France's withdrawal from Nato, or in America's exasperated withdrawal from Europe. Khrushchev would not remain the silent spectator of this tournament.

CHAPTER 15

LITTLE ENGLAND, GREAT BRITAIN

'*TOUTE ma vie je me faisais une certaine idée de la France*': thus General de Gaulle, in the opening words of his *War Memoirs*. What is that *certaine idée*?

The emotional side of me tends to imagine France, like the princess in the fairy story or the Madonna in the frescoes, as dedicated to an exalted and exceptional destiny. If, in spite of this, mediocrity shows in her acts and deeds, it strikes me as an absurd anomaly, to be imputed to the faults of Frenchmen, not to the genius of the land.

France is not Frenchmen. France is an ideal, a symbol, a metaphysic. De Gaulle's *certaine idée* must be a scandal to the Anglo-Saxon. Indeed, as one reads on, it is as if de Gaulle had anticipated the scandal with a dry audacity. The appeal is not to sentiment alone, he says, but to reason:

The positive side of my mind also assures me that France is not really herself unless she is in the front rank; that only vast enterprises are capable of counter-balancing the ferments of disintegration inherent in her people; that our country, as it is, surrounded by the others, as they are, must aim high and hold itself straight on pain of mortal danger. In short, in my mind, France cannot be France without greatness.

What is patriotism? A virtue almost always but never quite out of fashion. Nothing is easier to ridicule. Yet the penalties are severe. Patriotism is not mocked. Scratched, the cosmopolitan reveals a jingo. 'We will not fight for King and country' voted the Oxford Union in the month when Hitler took power in Germany. A generation had acquired a label. Seven years later there was a different label: 'Never have so many owed so much to so few.' A new label for a new generation. Yet it was the same generation. Patriotism returns to mock those that mock her. A man can live without a religion, a wife, a profession, a hobby, a philosophy. It seems that a man cannot live without a country. His country may not resemble a princess in a fairy story. But he has of his country *une certaine idée*. In few will this image be as compelling and articulate as in a Churchill or a de Gaulle. But patriotism is the commonest of the virtues. The sophisticated may mock; the people understand. Yet the patriotism of the common man is not the patriotism of a Churchill or a de Gaulle. Nor is it a 'national purpose'. It is a stronger, more primitive, less articulate thing. Churchill drew on it after Dunkirk. But it was not this patriotism that found expression in his speeches: Churchill's patriotism was altogether more *gaulliste*. For the popular patriotism of 1940 there is another witness:

One cannot see the modern world as it is unless one recognizes the overwhelming strength of patriotism, national loyalty. In certain circumstances it can break down, at certain levels of civilization it does not exist, but as a *positive* force there is nothing to set beside it. Christianity and international socialism are as weak as straw in comparison with it. Hitler and Mussolini rose to power in their own country very largely because they could grasp this fact and their opponents could not.

What is English patriotism? Orwell speaks of 'the dislike which nearly all foreigners feel for our national way of life'. Why should this be? It is said that foreigners dislike England only because they misunderstand her. That is not Orwell's view in *England, Your England*. Foreigners understand her very well. They dislike England for what she is. And what is she? Orwell offers his own *certaine idée*:

When you come back to England from any foreign country, you have immediately the sensation of breathing a different air. Even in the first few minutes, dozens of small things conspire to give you this feeling. The beer is bitterer, the coins are heavier, the grass is greener, the advertisements are more blatant. The crowds in the big towns, with their mild knobby faces, their bad teeth and gentle

manners are different from a European crowd. . . . There is some
thing distinctive and recognizable in English civilization. . .
What can the England of 1940 have in common with the England
of 1840? But then, what have you in common with the child o
five whose photographs your mother keeps on the mantelpiece?
Nothing, except that you happen to be the same person.

Orwell does not set out to flatter. That is not what patriot
ism is about. If you are born in England, you belong to her
for better or for worse. A country is not something one
chooses: it is a fate. In Orwell's view, then, the character
istics of the English are neither admirable nor contemptible
they simply are. One characteristic is that 'the English are
not gifted artistically'. Another that 'the English are not in
tellectual'. On the other hand, the English have 'a certain
power of acting without taking thought'. Orwell insists on
the '*privateness* of English life':

> We are a nation of flower-lovers, but also a nation of stamp
> collectors, pigeon-fanciers, amateur-carpenters, coupon-snippers
> darts-players, crossword-puzzle fans. All the culture that is mos
> truly native centres around things which even when they are
> communal are not official – the pub, the football match, the back
> garden, the fireside, and the 'nice cup of tea'. The liberty of the
> individual is still believed in, almost as in the nineteenth century
> . . . Like all other modern peoples, the English are in process o
> being numbered, labelled, conscripted. But the pull of their
> impulses is in the other direction and the kind of regimentation
> that can be imposed on them will be modified in consequence. No
> Party rallies, no Youth Movement, no coloured shirts, no Jew
> baiting or 'spontaneous' demonstrations. No Gestapo either, in al
> probability.

Certainly, there are foreign misconceptions about the English. Thus they are not at all puritanical:

> They are inveterate gamblers, drink as much beer as their wage
> will permit, are devoted to bawdy jokes, and use probably the
> foulest language in the world.

Nor, in spite of what foreigners think, are they religious
though

they have retained a deep tinge of Christian feeling while almost forgetting the name of Christ. The power worship which is the new religion of Europe and which has infected the English intelligentsia has never touched the common people.

They are, as foreigners have always said, hypocritical. But hypocrisy is the other face of a 'deeply moral attitude to life'. To Orwell, this finds expression in 'the gentleness of English civilization ... perhaps its most marked characteristic'. The English hate war and militarism; even their police carry no revolvers. Their favourite patriotic poems celebrate disasters, not victories. Another trait is their 'respect for constitution and legality'. The English are incurably insular. The English working class are 'outstanding in their abhorrence of foreign habits'. Orwell admits that

> The insularity of the English, their refusal to take foreigners seriously, is a folly that has to be paid for very heavily from time to time. But it plays its part in the English mystique, and the intellectuals who have tried to break it down have generally done more harm than good. At bottom it is the same quality in the English character that repels the tourist and keeps out the invader.

Orwell's English are insular, inartistic, unmilitary, unphilosophical. 'But this is perhaps,' Orwell adds, 'only another way of saying that the English are outside the European culture.' On this point, Orwell and the General think alike. Indeed, de Gaulle's *Memoirs* confirm Orwell on other points. De Gaulle did not like us; but he could admire what he disliked. Orwell's point about English *privateness* is not missed:

> I can see again my life at that time ... The ordinary people round about us preserved a sympathetic discretion. The attitude of the English when they saw me with my family passing along the streets, taking a walk in the park or going to a cinema, was as kindly reserved as the demonstrations were fervent when I appeared in public. So I was able, to my advantage, to verify that, among this great people, each one respects the liberty of the others.

Set against the humiliations of his life among the English, it is a generous and touching tribute. Sadly, de Gaulle contrasts English solidarity in defeat with the wretchedness of his fellow French. To de Gaulle, as to Orwell, English insularity implies no judgement: it is a fact of nature. Nor do they disagree about the innate patriotism of the English. There was no English characteristic de Gaulle more admired. Orwell wrote that, in England,

> up to a point, the sense of national unity is a substitute for a 'world view'. Just because patriotism is all but universal . . . there can be moments when the whole nation suddenly swings together and does the same thing, like a herd of cattle facing a wolf. There was such a moment, unmistakably, at the time of the disaster in France.

Does this mean that the instinct of the English will always tell them to do the right thing?

Not at all, merely that it will tell them to do the same thing. In the 1931 General Election, for instance, we all did the wrong thing in perfect unison . . . we were as single-minded as the Gadarene swine. . . . However much one may hate to admit it, it is almost certain that between 1931 and 1940 the National Government represented the will of the mass of the people. It tolerated slums, unemployment, and a cowardly foreign policy. Yes, but so did public opinion.

Why did the English people tolerate appeasement, and who opposed it? Earlier, I argued that appeasement was opposed by two groups in English life: the Churchillian Right, and the anti-Fascist Left. Orwell supports this view, though with reservations. He says of the anti-Churchill Right:

> The ruling class decayed, lost its ability, its daring, and finally its ruthlessness, until the time came when stuffed shirts like Eden or Halifax could stand out as men of exceptional talent. . . . What was it that at every decisive moment made every British statesman do the wrong thing with so unerring an instinct? *They could not struggle against Nazism or Fascism, because they could not understand. Neither could they have struggled against communism, if communism had been a serious force in Western Europe* . . . They are not wicked, or altogether wicked: they are merely unteachable. [My italics.]

His opinion of the left-wing intelligentsia is harsher. The middle class was losing its imperial instincts, Orwell admits but the general weakening of imperialism, and to some extent of the whole British morale, that took place during the nineteen-thirties was partly the work of the left-wing intelligentsia. . . . Many intellectuals of the Left were flabbily pacifist up to 1935, shrieked for war against Germany in the years 1935–9, and then promptly cooled off when the war started . . . England is perhaps the only great country where the intellectuals are ashamed of their own nationality. . . . If the English people suffered for several years a real weakening of morale, so that the Fascist nations judged that they were 'decadent' and that it was safe to plunge into war, the intellectual sabotage from the left was partly responsible. Both the *New Statesman* and the *News Chronicle* cried out against the Munich settlement, but even they had done something to make it possible.

Nevertheless, wrote Orwell in 1940, when the issue was still in doubt,

in whatever shape England emerges from the war, it will be deeply tinged with the characteristics I have spoken of. The intellectuals who hope to see it Russianized or Germanized will be disappointed. The gentleness, the hypocrisy, the thoughtlessness, the reverence for law, the hatred of uniforms will remain, along with the suet puddings and the misty skies. The Stock Exchange will be pulled down, the country houses will be turned into children's holiday camps, the Eton and Harrow match will be forgotten, but England will still be England, an everlasting animal stretching into the future and the past, and, like all living things, having the power to change out of all recognition and yet remain the same.

England, Your England was written twenty-three years ago. Yet Orwell's *certaine idée* has not dated. It is still the average Englishman's image of his country. Indeed, Orwell's essay has had a stranger fate. England and Orwell's image of her have not grown apart: on the contrary, England has grown to resemble Orwell's portrait of her. 'The crowds in the big cities, with their mild, knobby faces' are still with us. We meet them in the pages of Richard Hoggart's *The Uses of Literacy*, of Alan Sillitoe's *Saturday Night and Sunday Morning*. Unmistakably, it is Orwell's England that these writers celebrate. The England of Colin MacInnes's novels, of Arnold Wesker's plays, of Lindsay Anderson's films is Orwell's

Little England. Insular, amateurish, beer-drinking, hypocritical, foul-mouthed, unphilosophical: we grow more like
ourselves every day. We still do not do the right thing; but
we still do it in perfect unison. We are flexible when we
should be firm, firm when we should be flexible. We abuse
our friends; we love our enemies. In 1940, when Orwell
wrote *England, Your England*, it must have seemed that there
was one mistake the English could never make again:
Munich. Yet, twenty years later, the same wishful thinking
that justified appeasement of Hitler justified appeasement
of Khrushchev. *Plus ça change, plus c'est la même chose.* We are
not *perfide Albion*: we are merely unteachable.

As far as morality is concerned, Russians of the kind we met
appear to be less selfish and greedy than we are, genuinely devoted
to the public good, and still unfaltering in their sense of purpose
and in their confidence in their chosen values.

An excerpt from an English intellectual's Russian diary in
the nineteen-thirties? The tone is surely unmistakable – who
ever spoke of the United States in this tone? But no, the date
of the passage is the date of writing: March the first, nineteen
hundred and sixty-three; the journal is the *New Statesman*;
the writer Miss Jacquetta Hawkes.

England is Orwell's England, Little England. General de
Gaulle is quite right: the English will never make Europeans. Should that be the conclusion? Personally, I think
not. Orwell's up-to-dateness is astonishing; but is it not also
alarming? I too warm to Orwell's image of England: it is
an acceptable patriotism. Yet how extraordinary that we
should look to the England of 1940, of all possible Englands,
for our *certaine idée*! How right must those foreigners be who
see in our nostalgia the source of our troubles! For our nostalgia is unique. It has no equivalent in the mentality of
Russia, Germany, France, America. Which other great industrial society could have produced *The Uses of Literacy*
or *Saturday Night and Sunday Morning*? Certainly, there are
worse nostalgias, as there are worse patriotisms. Indeed, the

particular nostalgia with which foreigners charge us is absent.
Where is Britain's 'nostalgia for empire'? Indeed, where is
'Britain'? Orwell does not use the word: he speaks only of
England and the English. It is a revealing distinction. For
Britain too is *une certaine idée*. Britain is England at large,
England as empire, England as a world power: *Great* Britain.
In 1940, England still had these attributes. Indeed, it was
these attributes which the Nazis envied: to inherit them they
were determined to destroy her. That is how Churchill too saw
the struggle. But where Churchill spoke of Britain, Orwell
spoke of England. Do other peoples speak of themselves with
such ambiguity? I believe those who put down our troubles
to our nostalgia for empire miss this ambiguity. The loss of
empire has hurt us profoundly. Yet it entered our consciousness, while we still had it, far less than foreigners believe.
Orwell touches on this. To foreigners, he says, this nonchalant
attitude to empire is the last word in English hypocrisy. Yet
Orwell surely is right. For the majority of Englishmen there
never was such a thing as British patriotism. The ambiguity
expresses a paradox: John Bull, who ruled the greatest empire in history, was always a Little Englander at heart.

What is the prospect for John Bull? If what I say is true,
it ought not to be discouraging. Why should John Bull fret
if his empire has 'exhausted the mandate of heaven'? That
was not where his deepest loyalties lay. Why should he fear
to be confined to an island, if his heart never left it? Why
should John Bull not be happy in insularity? There are
many who believe that this is possible. Personally, I believe
that it is not. For it does violence to the ambiguity: John
Bull's island is both Little England and Great Britain: Orwell's English are lazy, feckless, pleasure-loving, unambi-
tious: there is hardly room among them for a Cromwell, a
Clive, a Nelson, a Churchill. These names evoke the ludi-
crous patriotism of the school-room. But the heroic virtues,
like patriotism, are not mocked. The mediocrities of Weimar
lead to the windy Valhallas of Nazism. There is a case nearer
to hand. There are enough Englishmen who cannot forgive

France for having de Gaulle for her leader. This is not a party-political book. I risk no predictions. But I would point to a danger. 'Talented as are Mr X and Mr Y, and even Mr Z,' the new cry will go, 'what Britain needs is a General de Gaulle.' Britain's post-war hesitations spring from the dilemmas that confront her in the world. Britain has been allowed to become the passive victim of these dilemmas, and lost much of her self-confidence. In this situation, the cry is for the man who can master dilemmas and not be mastered by them. I believe future governments will need to explain Britain's dilemmas frankly, and provide her with strong leadership. Otherwise, that cry will be increasingly heard in Britain.

It would be a counsel of despair. Fortunately, it is not likely to come about – if only because no de Gaulle is in sight. Still, I believe that demands for 'strong leadership' and a 'national purpose' will grow. I have said that the notion of a national purpose is self-contradictory. Those who have it do not speak of it; those who speak of it do not have it. This may not be true of more articulate peoples. But it is true of ourselves. Not the Germans, argues Orwell, but the English fit Hitler's famous description: 'a nation of sleepwalkers'. Sensing the demand for a sense of purpose, the democratic politician will respond. But if he responds with a gimmick, he is less to blame than his public. For to *demand* national purpose is to demand the impossible. Governments that are eloquent about national purpose are not often democratic. The issue should be squarely faced. Democratic governments exist to interpret the will of the people: they take their orders from the nation. But what if the will of the people is to receive orders, not to give them? A people that wants to receive orders, not to give them, no longer wants democratic government. Behind the demand for national purpose is the wish to escape from difficult dilemmas, to evade responsibility. Essentially, it is a demand for dictatorship. This is implicit in our fixation on 1940. What, after all, was the political pattern of 1940? There was national purpose, certainly. But the nation was in a state of siege. Social conflicts were in abeyance. There was a truce in the party struggle. The government had quasi-dictatorial powers. All this was necessary. But a democracy cannot reproduce this idyll in time of peace without ceasing to be a democracy. In part, the nostalgia for 1940 is nostalgia for a Churchillian Great Britain that 'must aim high and hold herself straight, on pain of mortal danger' – a *gaulliste* Britain that cannot be Britain without *grandeur*. But it is also a nostalgia for a Little England where the natural conflicts between classes, individuals, interests, and parties are in abeyance. It is a utopian vision, based on an imaginary idyll, whose actual terror is forgotten. Ostensibly, it is a democratic vision. But it could only be realized in a dictatorship.

I have suggested that the root of our troubles was a misreading of Dunkirk. Dunkirk meant the physical expulsion of Britain from Europe; it created the siege mentality to which I have alluded; it threw us back on our own resources. When the war was won, it was still 1940 we preferred to remember. The reason is plain. In 1940 we still bore the heat and burden of the day; by 1945 were the junior partner in a grand coalition. Victory, then, confirmed us in the attitudes of 1940. Few things in post-war Britain do not have their roots in that ill-remembered idyll. There is the insularity of our intellectual life compared with the decades before 1940. The first to profit, politically, was Labour in the 1945 election; in England's green and pleasant land must be built the classless socialist society first glimpsed in 1940. In the frustrations of austerity at home and Cold War abroad, the vision of Little England faded. It must be *Great* Britain again – and who better than Churchill to restore Britain's greatness? It is between these two poles – the placid social idyll of Little England and the thoughtless heroics of Great Britain – that British politics have moved since 1945.

These attitudes cut across party-political frontiers. The Labour Party is not *only* the party of Little England; the Conservative Party not *only* the party of Great Britain. Let me repeat: this is not a party-political book. My own sympathies are with the Left. But, if I am to be objective, I must admit that Labour and Conservative behaviour towards Europe, towards the Commonwealth, towards the Cold War, run to a common pattern. I do not mean that it is a matter of indifference which party is in power: I believe that Labour could provide more vigorous government at home. But in foreign affairs? Certainly, the Labour Party can no longer claim a monopoly of decolonialization: there is little room here for disagreement. Again, both parties have shown the same ambivalence towards Europe in the past. Nor is Labour government necessarily 'softer on communism'. On the contrary, experience shows that Labour is always under pressure to take a strong British stand; it is more easily accused of neglecting national security and appeasing foreigners. The pressures on a Conservative government are the reverse. It is when the Left is in opposition that neutralism and pacifism raise their heads. And the more popular a policy of appeasement with the electorate, the greater the temptation to steal the Left's clothes. It is no accident that the appeasement both of Hitler and of Khrushchev took place under Conservative administrations.

Both Little England and Great Britain are a misreading of Dunkirk. Dunkirk meant Britain's expulsion from Europe. But it did not mean Britain could live without Europe; it meant, on the contrary, that Britain could not live apart from Europe. The tragedy of Dunkirk was that it strengthened our insularity where it ought to have destroyed it once and for all. De Gaulle's rejection of our European credentials was based on a shrewd estimate of our mentality. De Gaulle was as right in his estimate, I fear, as he was wrong in the decision he took. Nonetheless, the decision is taken. Our entry into the Common Market is blocked, not permanently, but for many years. At the same time, the Common Market itself has declined in political significance. I do not believe the Commonwealth is a serious alternative, either politically, economically, or militarily. Nor do I believe we should apply to become the fifty-first state of the Union. Evidently, de Gaulle expects Britain to continue her slow, peevish, but untragic decline during the decade ahead. No doubt, in that subtle and magnanimous heart, there is a corner of regret: '*Ne pleurez plus, milord,*' he is said to have comforted Britain's Prime Minister at Rambouillet. But I doubt if that is his real opinion. I doubt if General de Gaulle, like Hitler and Napoleon (those petty minds with whom he is falsely compared), underrates us in that way.

He may take a poor view of our economic prospects. But when was de Gaulle ever interested in economics? It is political power that concerns him. Here, the *Memoirs* suggest a different reading. It is because he sees in us his only serious rival for the leadership of Europe that he is determined to exclude us. But if it is a political battle to shape Europe's future we are engaged in, our prospects are at once much better. We have a strong bargaining counter: our nuclear superiority. In the background there is the still greater superiority of the United States. Bearing in mind de Gaulle's thinking on the subject, and the likely weakness of the French *force de frappe*, it is a formidable political advantage. We shall have to seek new friends in Scandinavia, Holland, Turkey, Italy, Spain, Japan. In particular, we shall have to give up our suicidal anti-Germanism – indeed, we shall have to see in Germany our chief ally against French hegemony in Europe. There will have to be a revision of our attitude to the Cold War. I have argued that the very structure of Europe – her domination by four powers of equal size – means that a hegemony of one of these three powers must always be unstable. That is a powerful factor in our favour. What we must aim for is not the 'leadership' of Europe: Europe is looking for an equal partnership with a democratic Britain, not for a British de Gaulle. What we should aim for is an equal place for Britain in a directorium of Europe's major powers. It is a more modest prospect for John Bull than some he has been offered; but I believe it is the only realistic one. *Faisons-nous l'Europe!*

A SHORT BIBLIOGRAPHY

Allen, H. C. *The Anglo-American Predicament.* (Macmillan)
Beaton, Leonard, and Maddox, John. *The Spread of Nuclear Weapons.* (Chatto & Windus)
Bell, Coral. *Negotiation from Strength.* (Chatto & Windus)
Brimmell, J. H. *Communism in South-East Asia.* (Oxford)
Brumberg, Abraham. *Russia under Khrushchev.* (Methuen)
Conquest, Robert. *Commonsense about Russia.* (Gollancz)
Crankshaw, Edward. *Khrushchev's Russia.* (Penguin)
Crossman, R. H. S. *The Charm of Politics.* (Hamish Hamilton)
Dallin, Alexander. *The Soviet Union and the United Nations.* (Methuen)
Dallin, David. *Soviet Foreign Policy after Stalin.* (Methuen)
Deutscher, Isaac. *The Great Contest.* (Oxford)
de Gaulle, Charles. *War Memoirs.* (Weidenfeld & Nicolson)
Halle, Louis. *American Foreign Policy.* (Allen & Unwin)
Heilbrunn, Otto. *Partisan Warfare.* (Allen & Unwin)
Kahn, Herman. *On Thermonuclear War.* (Oxford)
    Thinking about the Unthinkable. (Weidenfeld & Nicolson)
Kennan, George. *Russia and the West under Lenin and Stalin.* (Hutchinson)
Kissinger, Henry. *Nuclear Weapons and Foreign Policy.* (Harper)
    The Necessity for Choice. (Chatto & Windus)
Labedz, Leopold. *Revisionism.* (Allen & Unwin)
Lichtheim, George. *Europe and America.* (Thames & Hudson)
Liddell Hart, B. H. *Deterrence or Defence?* (Stevens)
Mayne, Richard. *The Community of Europe.* (Gollancz)
Orwell, George. *The Lion and the Unicorn.* (Secker & Warburg)
Osanka, Franklin Mark. *Modern Guerilla Warfare.* (Free Press of Glencoe).
Rose, Saul. *Britain and South-East Asia.* (Chatto & Windus)
Shapiro, Leonard. *The Communist Party of the Soviet Union.* (Eyre & Spottiswoode)
Seton-Watson, Hugh. *Neither War nor Peace.* (Methuen)
    The Pattern of Communist Revolution. (Methuen)
Shanks, Michael. *The Stagnant Society.* (Penguin)
    Britain and the New Europe. (Chatto & Windus)
Strachey, John. *End of Empire.* (Gollancz)
    On the Prevention of War. (Macmillan)
Tanham, George K. *Communist Revolutionary Warfare.* (Methuen)
Ward, Barbara. *India and the West.* (Hamish Hamilton)
Wood, Neal. *Communism and British Intellectuals.* (Gollancz)
Woodhouse, C. M. *British Foreign Policy since the Second World War.* (Hutchinson)